DID YOU KN⬚
YOU CAN TAKE ON THE CHALLENGE
WITH YOUR WHOLE CHURCH?

ALL-IN, TURNKEY SERMON SERIES WITH PROVEN RESULTS!

WWW.SERVINGCHALLENGE.COM/CHURCH

WANT YOUR PASTOR TO RECEIVE A FREE COPY?
EMAIL HELLO@REDLETTERCHALLENGE.COM

ACKNOWLEDGMENTS

You'll never read a book written by the best servants. They are all too busy doing the actual serving to be bothered about writing about it. My dad, Roger Buck, is one of those people. Serving is how he loved. Dad, I want to learn to serve people the way you do. Thanks for showing me that true servanthood is a life spent pointing people to Jesus.

Many other servants need to be thanked for this book:

Zach, my life partner, boss, and our fearless leader. Your dedicated service to Jesus sets the tone for all that we do. I love being on this journey with you.

Doug Peterson, co-author and editor. You always go above and beyond what is expected with a humble servant's heart. You truly make the books come alive in every way. We couldn't do it without you.

Andrea Miller, our operations director, your service is unmatched! Without your enthusiasm, encouragement, and dedication to advancing God's kingdom, we would not be where we are today!

Steve and Susan Blount, our team from Blount Collective, you are dedicated to advancing the kingdom by serving Christians around the world of all denominations and walks of life. We are grateful for your partnership.

And our sons, Nathan and Brady, who help us practice what we preach!

Jesus never wrote a single letter down in all of His ministry. Instead, as the truest picture of a servant, He spent His life doing the most important thing: being a servant to all.

— ALLISON ZEHNDER

TABLE OF
CONT

ENTS

BOUND FOR THE PROMISED LAND

Harriet Tubman and her two brothers were lost in a dark forest.

Harriet convinced two of her brothers, Henry and Benjamin, to escape from slavery on the night of September 15, 1849. But they soon became lost in the deep woods of Maryland and trudged back to bondage. Back to slavery.

Two days later, Harriet tried to escape once again, this time alone. When she spotted the master, Mr. Thompson, approaching on horseback, Harriet sensed God telling her to pick up and leave at that very moment. So, Harriet walked straight at Mr. Thompson and began singing these words:

> *"I'll meet you in the morning,*
> *Safe in the Promised Land,*
> *On the other side of Jordan,*
> *Bound for the Promised Land!"*

As she sang, Harriet walked past Mr. Thompson, who stopped and stared. What could be going through the man's mind? Did he know she was escaping? Did he wonder why she was singing about the Promised Land?

Harriet Tubman strolled through the gate and kept on walking, eventually reaching freedom. It was a miracle! Mr. Thompson didn't even try to stop her. She had escaped!

THE UNDERGROUND RAILROAD

Harriet Tubman went on to become the most famous "conductor" on the Underground Railroad. This was not a real railroad with trains and tracks. The Underground Railroad was a string of houses, stretching from the South to the North in the United States. Escaping slaves fled from house to house as they traveled from slavery in the South to freedom in the North. The people leading the escaped slaves along this Underground Railroad were known as conductors.

These people could also be called "servants." After all, servants put other people's needs ahead of their own. They're willing to make sacrifices for others.

Harriet Tubman and other conductors risked their lives to help people reach freedom. And although Harriet reached freedom in the North, that didn't stop her from going back into danger in the South to rescue others. God guided her path.

Harriet was a devoted follower of Jesus, who was the ultimate servant. Jesus laid down His life so we too could find freedom. This is a book that will help you learn to serve like Jesus. As it says in the Bible…

"This is how we know what love is: Jesus Christ laid down his life for us. And we ought to lay down our lives for our brothers and sisters. If anyone has material possessions and sees a brother or sister in need but has no pity on them, how can the love of God be in that person?" 1 John 3:16-17 (NIV)

Loving someone means serving them. In this book, we will not only look at how Jesus served us, but you will have a chance to be a servant yourself.

SERVANTS AND SLAVES

Slaves and servants are very different. While servants do things for others freely, slaves have no choice. They are property. People own them and have total control.

In many cases, slaves were not even allowed to learn how to read—although some Christians in America broke this rule and taught slaves how to read the Bible. Slavery is against the law in most countries today, but that doesn't stop it from happening.

Serving others is much different from slavery because it is a choice. It's something we do out of love. It's something we do because Jesus showed us the way. Not only did Jesus serve us, but He died for us. His death was a world-changing event.

Jesus is not like a master or a king of long ago who mistreats his slaves. On the contrary, He wants to set us free. We are slaves to sin, and Jesus seeks to break our chains. But to do that, Jesus had to give up a lot. In fact, Philippians says He became like a slave when He became a human.

Imagine! The King of the Universe became like a slave. That's why His life and death flipped the world upside down. Human kings do not set aside their crowns to become servants or slaves. But Jesus did!

Jesus's death was the most upside-down act ever, and it changed everything for the better.

> **"When the time came, he [Jesus] set aside the privileges of deity and took on the status of a slave, became *human*! Having become human, he stayed human. It was an incredibly humbling process. He didn't claim special privileges. Instead, he lived a selfless, obedient life and then died a selfless, obedient death—and the worst kind of death at that—a crucifixion." Philippians 2:7-8 (MSG)**

In *Serving Challenge Kids*, we want you to stop thinking only about yourself and take time to make someone else's life better. We also want you to study the actions of the greatest servant of all time—Jesus.

THE WAY

Following Jesus is like hiking through a forest. It's easy to get lost in the woods, just as it's easy to lose your way in life. But if you have an expert guide, you can make it through the deepest, darkest forest—just as Harriet Tubman led escaped slaves through the forests of Maryland

In life, Jesus is our expert guide. He is our conductor on a spiritual Underground Railroad that carries us through a dark woods on the way to glorious freedom. Jesus is the Way. That's why the first Christians were called "followers of the Way."

After all, it isn't only important to *believe* in Jesus. It's vital we *follow* Him. We must follow the Way, or we'll be sure to get lost in the woods. He is like our North Star, which escaping slaves followed to guide them north.

TREES THAT TEACH

Throughout this book, we will talk a lot about trees because they are an ideal symbol of servanthood. Trees serve us in many ways. They provide shade in the heat. They give us wood to build houses and ships. They hold the soil firmly in place. Trees give.

Trees even serve other trees, as we will discover. They communicate with each other through the underground network of roots and fungi. You might even say that trees have their own Underground Railroad.

So, get ready to hike through the woods and explore the mystery of trees as we learn about servanthood and following the Way. The first five days of the 40-day challenge will introduce us to the five biggest questions about how Jesus served. Then, in the next 35 days, we'll dig deeper into those five questions.

You've heard of the Fantastic Four? Well, think of these questions as the Fantastic Five.

DAYS 6–12: WHY DID JESUS SERVE?

This section is all about our attitude, or mindset—how we think about serving. Our attitude is like the **SEEDS** from which a tree grows and the **ROOTS** that hold it in place.

> **"In your relationships with one another, have the same mindset as Christ Jesus…" Philippians 2:5 (NIV)**

DAYS 13–19: WHEN DID JESUS SERVE?

Jesus was never too busy to serve others, and He didn't think He was too important to help. He served, even at the worst times, such as in the midst of storms and trials. Taking time to serve is how we connect to others, just like a tree **TRUNK** connects the roots with the branches and leaves. The trunk holds a tree together, and Jesus does the same for us during the storms in our life.

> **"…Who, being in very nature God, did not consider equality with God something to be used to his own advantage; rather, he made himself nothing…" Philippians 2:6-7a (NIV)**

DAYS 20–26: HOW DID JESUS SERVE?

This section is all about actions—what did Jesus do to serve people? When He became a human and walked the land of Israel, where did He go and how did He serve? Our actions are like a tree's **BRANCHES**, which carries food to the leaves.

> **"…by taking the very nature of a servant, being made in human likeness." Philippians 2:7b (NIV)**

DAYS 27–33: WHO DID JESUS SERVE?

When Jesus died, He died for all of us. The people we serve are like a tree's **LEAVES**, which receive the nutrients passing through the tree. The leaves grow in the spring and turn spectacular colors in the fall. They're as beautiful as the people we serve.

> **"And being found in appearance as a man, he humbled himself by becoming obedient to death—even death on a cross!" Philippians 2:8 (NIV)**

DAYS 34–40: WHAT DID JESUS DO BY SERVING?

Jesus gave us freedom from sin and life that lasts forever. This eternal life is like the delicious **FRUIT** of a tree. When Jesus was crucified, the cross was made from the wood of a tree—a Giving Tree. He served us by making the greatest, most important sacrifice in the history of the world. And the fruit of His sacrifice is forgiveness and redemption.

> **"Therefore God exalted him to the highest place and gave him the name that is above every name, that at the name of Jesus every knee should bow, in heaven and on earth and under the earth, and every tongue acknowledge that Jesus Christ is Lord, to the glory of God the Father." Philippians 2:9-11 (NIV)**

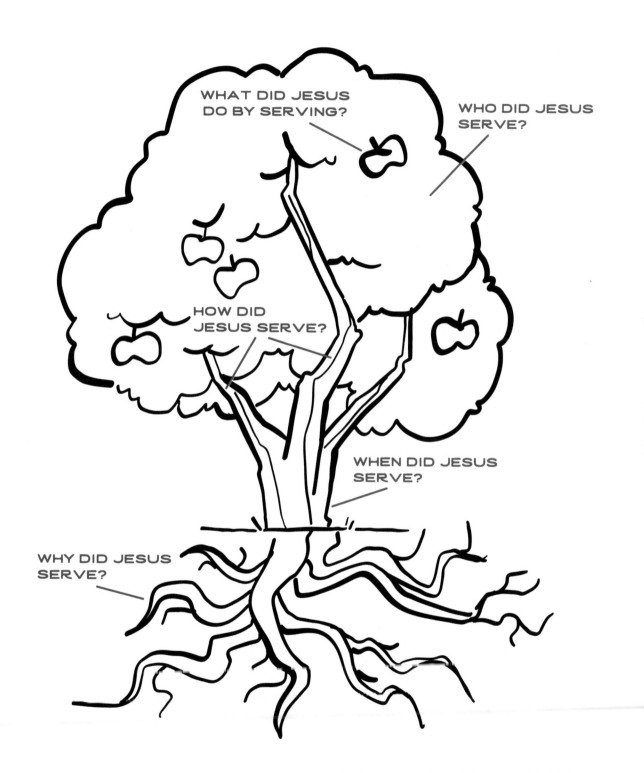

THE FOREST OF REDVALE

In our last three books, *Red Letter Challenge Kids*, *Being Challenge Kids*, and *Forgiving Challenge Kids*, you met Aiden, Isabella, and Emily Perez as they ventured to an incredible land called Redvale. The three Perez kids are back in this book with an all-new adventure that will build on the lessons we learn in *Serving Challenge Kids*.

The story begins on page 15 and continues throughout the book. To dig deeper, check out discussion questions for *The Forest of Redvale* at:

WWW.SERVINGCHALLENGE.COM/FREE-KIDS-RESOURCES

RED ALERTS!

One of the characters in *The Forest of Redvale* is Red, a fox who speaks three languages. Scattered throughout the book, you'll find brief Red Alerts from Red the Fox, offering nuggets of information about the Bible.

FIND TEAMMATES

Finally, *Serving Challenge Kids* was created to be experienced with others as a family, class, Sunday School, or youth group. We encourage you to find somebody with whom you can embark on this adventure. So, pick up your walking stick and enter the forest. Let your 40 days begin now!

THE FOREST OF REDVALE

PART 1

Isabella Perez lay around like a bump on a log. She curled on the couch, glued to her phone. She texted friends, scrolled through photos, scanned posts, and checked on her number of "likes." These days, Isabella's finger was the only part of her body getting exercise as she swiped it across the screen, again and again.

Emily, her little sister, darted into the living room. "C'mon, Isabella! Today is the church food drive! Let's go!"

Emily grabbed her sister's foot and tried to drag her from the couch. But she would've had better luck pulling down a giant redwood. Isabella was rooted to the cushions.

Deep down, Isabella knew she should get up and do something. But she couldn't take her eyes off her screen. Scrolling on screens was so much easier than working at a church food drive. At church, she would be filling bags with canned goods and boxes of food as one person after another shuffled through the line.

Boring!

"I'm staying home today," Isabella said. "Maybe next month."

"You're going!" Emily commanded. "Besides, isn't your screen time over?"

"You aren't my boss," Isabella said, even though she knew she had been on her phone longer than allowed.

Just then, their brother, Aiden, bolted through the room, and Emily turned her fury on him. "And where do you think you're going? Aren't you helping with the food drive?"

Aiden stopped, as if he had been lassoed. "Sorry, sis, but I've got basketball practice in an hour. Maybe next month I can help out."

"But that's what you said last month. It seems like you've got practices all day, every day. If you—"

"Gotta get my stuff," Aiden said, and just like that he vanished.

Emily whirled around and returned her fury to Isabella. "You're not off the hook. I'll be back in a second to get you. We can bike to the church."

Don't make eye contact, and she'll go away, Isabella thought, staring at her phone and swiping the screen. *Swipe, swipe, swipe.* Sure enough, after a few minutes, Isabella looked up and Emily was gone. She sighed. Finally, some peace and quiet.

Isabella burrowed deeper into the couch, getting more comfortable. *Swipe, swipe, swipe.* Her finger worked away, flicking across her phone as image after image flashed by.

Suddenly, the picture of a fox popped up on her phone. But not just any fox. It was Red the Fox, their friend from the land of Redvale. They hadn't seen him for almost six months.

Isabella's heart nearly stopped because whenever they saw Red the Fox, that usually meant trouble. She was not in the mood for this kind of grief, so she swiped the screen—but there was Red the Fox again. This time, he appeared in a video on her phone.

"Wait, Isabella! Hear me out!" the fox shouted.

Swipe! Isabella swiped her screen, but Red was still there, pleading with her.

"Isabella, we're in trouble!"

Isabella powered down her phone. She was terrified of what Red might be asking them to do now. The last time, they nearly died in a volcano!

Breathing heavily, Isabella reached for her laptop. If she couldn't use her phone, she'd go to her computer. But when she brought up MeTube, there was Red the Fox again, appearing in every video she came across.

"The trees are dying!" Red shouted. "Isabella, you need to get your brother and sister and come to Redvale this very—"

Isabella slammed down the lid of her laptop. Next, she reached for her iPad. But Red was waiting for her there as well.

"Don't shut me down!" Red said. "We need your help or—"

Isabella shut him down.

As she sat there, her heart racing, she knew she should find out what Red wanted. But she also knew it would be a dangerous mission, and she just hoped to relax and spend her day on her devices.

Unable to resist the lure of the screen, Isabella tried the TV. Surely, Red couldn't be on every streaming service!

He could.

Every time she clicked her remote, there was Red's face, filling the widescreen TV.

"Hey! What's Red doing on TV?" Emily shouted.

Isabella turned to see that both Emily and Aiden had entered the living room.

"It's nothing." Isabella clicked her remote, but Red was still there on the big screen.

"Give that to me!" Aiden shouted, wrestling the remote out of her clutches. But Isabella didn't want to give it up. It was as if the remote controlled her, like the Ring of Power. *My preciousssssssss!*

Aiden was stronger, so he eventually pried the remote from her fingers and turned up the volume on the TV.

"What's going on, Red?" Emily said, standing directly in front of the TV, hands on hips.

"I'm glad you asked," said Red. "I've been trying to get Isabella's attention for fifteen minutes now!"

Emily cut a nasty glance at Isabella.

"The trees in the Forest of Redvale are dying!" said the fox. "We need your help!"

"What's causing it?" Aiden asked. "Is it the Destroyers?"

In Redvale, there was a constant battle between the Destroyers and the forces of good.

"Yes, the Destroyers are at it again," said Red. "Leaves are wilting. Branches are breaking. Entire trees are falling. Some trees are turning to chaff and blowing away in the wind."

"What's chaff?" Emily asked.

Just then, a Bible verse popped into Isabella's head. In the last few months, she had stopped memorizing verses, but many of the words still floated around in her brain. The passage that flashed in her mind included the word "chaff," so she recited it.

"That person is like a tree planted by streams of water, which yields its fruit in season and whose leaf does not wither—whatever they do prospers. Not so the wicked! They are like chaff that the wind blows away."

Aiden blinked. "Huh?"

"That's from Psalm 1. I think 'chaff' is like dust," said Isabella.

"Bingo! That's right!" said Red, leaning forward so his entire face filled the TV screen. "Some of the trees are turning to dust!"

"But how can we get to Redvale?" Emily asked.

Isabella had enough of this. She snatched the remote from Aiden's hands, pointed it at the TV, and…

CLICK! POW!

Suddenly, there was a pop and brilliant burst of light. Isabella thought maybe their TV had exploded. The light was so bright that it blinded her for a few seconds. But when her vision finally cleared, the living room was gone. The TV was gone. So was the couch.

In their place was a forest. And standing two feet in front of her was Red the Fox.

"*That's* how you get to Redvale," he said.

TO BE CONTINUED ON PAGE 43.

THE FANTASTIC FIVE

1. WHY DID JESUS SERVE?
2. WHEN DID JESUS SERVE?
3. HOW DID JESUS SERVE?
4. WHO DID JESUS SERVE?
5. WHAT DID JESUS DO BY SERVING?

DAY 1
WHY DID JESUS SERVE? (BECAUSE HE'S GALLANT)

GOOFUS AND GALLANT

In the magazine *Highlights for Children*, you'll find a long-running comic strip about two boys named Goofus and Gallant. Gallant is always happy, kind, and respectful. Goofus is the opposite. He is selfish and rude. Below, can you pick which description is about **Goofus** and which is about **Gallant**?

_____TURNS ON THE TELEVISION WHEN THERE ARE GUESTS.

WHENEVER GUESTS ARRIVE, _____ TURNS OFF HIS SCREEN.

_____ GETS UP AND LETS HIS GRANDPA HAVE THE LA-Z-BOY.

_____ RUSHES TO FIND THE BEST SEAT FOR HIMSELF.

_____ STAYS IN THE KITCHEN TO EAT HIS SNACK.

_____EATS SNACKS ON THE LIVING ROOM CARPET.

_____SETS A TIMER, SO HE KNOWS WHEN SCREEN TIME IS OVER.

_____ HIDES IN THE CLOSET, SO HIS MOM WON'T KNOW HOW MUCH TIME HE USES HIS IPAD.

_____IS HAPPY TO PRAY AND IS THANKFUL FOR WHAT HE HAS.

_____WANTS TO SKIP PRAYER AT MEALTIME TO HURRY UP AND EAT.

The editor of *Highlights for Children* once said, "Kids see parts of themselves in both characters. No one is as good as Gallant, and no one is as bad as Goofus. But being more like Gallant is something to strive for."

The editor was right. It is important to try to make good choices like Gallant. But the Bible tells us about someone who was way better at good choices than Gallant. Jesus didn't just make good choices. He was *perfect*. As we follow Jesus, we need to copy how He did things. We need to copy His mindset, or attitude.

THE MINDSET OF JESUS

"In your relationships with one another, have the same mindset as Christ Jesus," says Philippians 2:5. Let's break down this verse into two parts.

PART ONE: "IN YOUR RELATIONSHIPS WITH ONE ANOTHER..."
Serving always includes other people. Your attitude affects not just you; it affects you and everyone around you. It is about you and others.

PART TWO: "...HAVE THE SAME MINDSET AS CHRIST JESUS."
Your attitude—how you feel and think—affects how you act. Having "the same mindset" means thinking and understanding things the way Jesus does.

God designed us to help others. In fact, scientists who study the brain found that helping people stimulates the same part of the brain as when we win a prize or eat a delicious meal. So, when people say serving feels good, they are right!

We can see Gallant in ourselves when we try to be good, kind, and loving— when we want to make the right choices. The problem is that we're not perfect. Therefore, we can also understand Goofus because we all make bad choices. No matter how much we try, we will not always get things right.

Jesus served us with a humble and correct attitude. When you look at Jesus's attitude, you see that:

- He loves the world. He sees it as a beautiful place that needs to be taken care of.

- He sees each person as worthwhile. No one is useless. Ever.

- No matter where you live, how healthy you are, or what you have, we are all broken and need fixing.

Believing these things starts you on the journey of being a servant. On Day 1, we're looking at our attitudes because this is where it all begins. Your attitude is like the seed, which is where a plant begins its life. If your attitude isn't in the right place, then serving will never happen. Because Jesus died for your goof-ups, you can follow your brave and gallant leader, Jesus!

CHALLENGE: HOW'S YOUR 'TUDE?

Mark "True" or "False" to check your attitudes about the poor.

The only way you are poor is if you don't have things or money.
True ☐ **False** ☐

The best way to help poor people is to give them money or things.
True ☐ **False** ☐

When I see a homeless or poor person, I think they must have done something wrong.
True ☐ **False** ☐

When someone has a nice home, clothes, food, toys, car, and other things, they are automatically happy.
True ☐ **False** ☐

Jesus is not present in poor or dangerous neighborhoods. That's where Satan exists.
True ☐ **False** ☐

I should feel guilty if I have a nice house and warm clothes and have never been hungry.
True ☐ **False** ☐

We don't need to listen to the people
we help. We know what is best for
them, and we decide how to help.
True ☐   **False** ☐

Donating food and clothes is great, but people need more than just stuff. Stuff
doesn't make us better. Jesus does. Many poor people feel ashamed, alone,
hopeless, powerless, and less valuable than others. But sometimes, you too can
feel these things, even if you have plenty of stuff. You can find Jesus in the poor
neighborhoods, rich areas, and everywhere in between.

The bottom line: You are not okay, and the people you want to help are not okay.
We all need Jesus because only He makes all things beautiful!

RED ALERT!

Joseph, the son of Jacob,
was gallant, for he rescued his family
from famine. Joseph was also compared
to a tree. Genesis 49:22 says, "Joseph
is a fruitful branch, a fruitful branch by
a spring; Its branches hang over a wall."
(NASB) His fruit was the service to his
family and his people.

DAY 2

WHEN DID JESUS SERVE? (AT THE RIGHT TIME)

THE JOURNEY

Refugees are people who leave their homes because of war or other terrible things. In 2021, for example, many Syrian refugees had to escape their country because war was tearing apart their homeland. Faez al Sharra was one such refugee, but he would not have been able to escape Syria if people hadn't helped him along the way.

One day, on his way home from work, the police held Faez at gunpoint and accused him of carrying a hidden gun. A stranger saw him with his hands in the air, so she pretended she was his mother and begged the soldiers to let him go. They eventually did.

After that scary encounter, Faez knew he was not safe in Syria. He packed up a few things and left with his wife and mother. A group of smugglers agreed to help them get across the border, but Faez and his wife had to hike ninety minutes in the pitch darkness to meet them.

That night, as they snuck through destroyed neighborhoods, a missile crashed into a nearby building. Things were getting worse, so they knew they had picked the right time to leave.

Faez finally made it to a refugee camp where he had to wait a long time for a new home.

For two years, Faez worked with many helpful organizations and people before he found a place to go. Still, when Faez heard that he could move to Texas in the United States, he was unsure. Texas seemed so far away, and he did not speak English.

When the time finally came to leave, Faez was scared because it was his first time on an airplane. After he arrived in the U.S., many people served Faez by helping him find a home and a job. He did not forget the acts of kindness when he escaped. Those small ways of helping saved his life.

Many people helped Faez get to a safe place because they were at the right place at the right time.

JUST SHOW UP

God is always at the right place at the right time. Read the entire Bible passage below. The first part is yesterday's verse, and the bold section is today's verse.

> "In your relationships with one another, have the same mindset as Christ Jesus: **Who, being in very nature God, did not consider equality with God something to be used to his own advantage; rather, he made himself nothing." Philippians 2:5-7a (NIV)**

When you serve, you put the needs of others before your own, which is what Jesus did. As the verse says, "he made himself nothing." That's another way of saying He gave up everything to serve us.

Jesus put the needs of others first by going where the people are. He traveled long distances on foot, going to busy synagogues, and he braved storms by riding in boats. He showed up to reach the people who were hurting or suffering.

When you serve others, be like Jesus. Just show up!

JUST LISTEN

Sometimes we want to help, but we spend so much time thinking, planning, and organizing that we never get around to doing anything. Instead, try doing something unplanned. It takes only one person making themselves available, like the woman who pretended to be Faez's mother.

Once you make yourself available to help, just listen. When we sit with people and listen to others, we notice what someone needs.

Also, helping is not always about things or money. Helping can be as simple as a smile or an invitation to your house.

OPEN OR CLOSED?

Have you ever gone to a store, only to find out that it just closed or isn't open yet? It's frustrating. People can be like closed stores. When you go to them for help, some make it clear they don't want to take the time. It's like they put up a "Closed" sign, sending you away, feeling sad or frustrated.

Serving means we are "open" to helping others. For example, little acts of kindness helped Faez escape from a dangerous situation. When we notice little things, we can help in big ways. "Open" your heart today!

CHALLENGE: OPEN FOR BUSINESS

Color the sign. Your challenge today is to tell someone that you are open and available to help. Who knows what they might ask you to do!

RED ALERT!

In the Bible, the first followers of Jesus were not called "Christians." That name did not come until later in the Book of Acts, which tells the story of the early Church. The first believers in the New Testament were called followers of "the Way." Jesus is the Way.

DAY 3

HOW DID JESUS SERVE? (BY SHOWING US THE WAY)

MAZE MADNESS

Today, we're going to learn about Jesus's actions when He served. But we're also going to find out about an extraordinary animal that took amazing actions to help others. First, help this ship get safely through the ocean maze below.

DOLPHIN DEEDS

You did a great job getting that ship through the maze! You're as incredible as a famous dolphin named Pelorus Jack.

Pelorus Jack, or Jack for short, was first spotted in 1888 guiding ships through a dangerous channel in New Zealand. Jack would swim alongside the ship for about twenty minutes, leading them past sharp rocks and tight corners. No one knew how Jack learned to do this, but ship captains began to trust him so much that if they did not see the dolphin, they would wait until he appeared. There wasn't a single shipwreck while he guided them.

In 1904, a sailor on the *SS Penguin* tried to shoot Jack, although the dolphin fortunately survived. When the New Zealand government found out, they passed a law to protect Jack. As a result, the incredible dolphin continued to guide ships through the channel—that is, every ship except the *SS Penguin*.

Without Jack's help, that ship had to make its way alone. Five years later, the SS Penguin sank in the channel after hitting a rock during a storm. It was a terrible accident. Seventy-five people drowned, and only thirty people survived. It was one of the worst maritime incidents in New Zealand's history.

The last time anyone saw Jack was in 1912. No one knows what happened to him, but he was twenty-four years old when he disappeared, so most people believed he died of old age.

IF A DOLPHIN CAN DO IT...

When God made the world, His plan was for people to work together and help each other. And if a dolphin can help others, so can we! But something messed up God's plan. Sin made us selfish, and now we often choose to think more about ourselves than others.

Some kids are too afraid or too busy to help. Serving others means you may have to give up something, such as your time or money. As a result, we often don't want to serve. But Jesus wants us to serve, even when we might not feel like it.

THE NATURE OF A SERVANT

Yesterday, we learned that Jesus made Himself nothing and gave up everything. Today, let's learn more about what that means. Read the entire passage below. We will focus on the last sentence in bold for today.

"In your relationships with one another, have the same mindset as Christ Jesus: Who, being in very nature God, did not consider equality with God something to be used to his own advantage; rather, he made himself nothing **by taking the very nature of a servant, being made in human likeness."**
Philippians 2:5-7 (NIV)

Let's break this verse down.

PART ONE: "...BY TAKING THE VERY NATURE OF A SERVANT..."
Jesus became a servant. He wasn't just wearing a servant costume and putting on an act. Jesus had a servant's heart on the inside. It was part of His nature.

PART TWO: "...BEING MADE IN HUMAN LIKENESS."
"Human likeness" means Jesus had an actual human body. Although He is God, Jesus chose to be born like all of us. His body was a lot like yours. If Jesus ran too hard, He got out of breath. He also got hungry, thirsty, or tired after a long day. Gravity caused Jesus to trip and scrape His knee, just like you.

One reason Jesus had a human body was so He could understand what it feels like for us to hurt. He had a heart for our hurts.

When you know what it feels like to be lonely, sad, or angry, you are more likely to want to help others who feel the same things. In fact, research has shown that when you hear or see someone else's pain, your nervous system responds much the same as when you feel your own pain. That's called feeling compassion.

The desire to show compassion is as much a part of you as the need to eat or breathe. This means you don't have to teach a person how to feel bad for someone else. Compassion comes naturally. So, when we see others sitting alone at lunch or a new teammate who doesn't know anyone, most of us want to help.

God gives us plenty of opportunities to serve. Most serving can happen right where you are, like Dolphin Jack in the New Zealand channel. When you see others in need, you can jump into action because you know the way through the rocky passage. And you know the way because Jesus is the Way.

In other words, when you serve others, you show them Jesus. And when you show them Jesus, you show them the Way.

CHALLENGE: GIVE DIRECTIONS

Look for an opportunity to help someone by giving them directions. For instance, meet a new neighbor and tell them how to find the nearest park or the best Fro-Yo shop...help someone looking for the shortest checkout line at the store...or greet a new visitor at church and offer to show them around.

When you know your way around, you can help others who may be lost. Remember, if a dolphin can do it, so can you.

DAY 4

WHO DID JESUS SERVE?
(EVERYONE, INCLUDING THE HOPELESS)

COMPLETELY HOPELESS

"Dad? Can you fill up the tub for me?" ten-year-old Nick asked. "I want to relax in the bath."

As Nick heard the tub filling, he looked around his bedroom. *This will be the last time I have to be here,* he thought. Relief washed over him. He would finally be free. All his life, he felt like a failure and believed he was no good. Completely hopeless, there was only one thing left to do.

Nick didn't want to relax in the bathtub.

Nick wanted to drown.

BORN DIFFERENT

Nick Vujicic was born in Australia with no arms or legs. Whenever he drew pictures of himself as a stick person, Nick would draw a lollipop: a body and head—but no arms and legs.

When Nick was born, his mother was too scared at first to hold or look at him because he was so different. After she recovered from the shock, Nick's parents took him home. They were Christians and believed that God had a plan for their son. They loved him and gave him the best childhood possible. But school was a nightmare.

Nick had a tough time accepting that he was different from others. Oftentimes, he could not participate in activities. Nick felt lonely and was bullied by some of the other kids. He thought his disability made him worthless, and that it would be better if he weren't alive.

ROOTED IN JESUS

Being rooted in anything other than Jesus leads to disappointment. Jesus is the only trustworthy source of hope and joy. Once Nick realized this, his whole life changed. Nick decided to let God decide what his abilities were, not other people. At age seventeen, Nick shared his faith at a prayer group, and he later started an organization called Life Without Limbs. Nick made it his mission to lift up anyone who would listen. Read what he said:

"... for every disability you have, you are blessed with more than enough abilities to overcome your challenges."

It didn't matter that Nick Vujicic didn't have arms or legs. He had a brain, eyes, ears, mouth, and body, so he refused to give up. He realized that when Jesus went to the cross, it was even harder than what he had to go through. Read the verses below, focusing on the words in bold.

"In your relationships with one another, have the same mindset as Christ Jesus: Who, being in very nature God, did not consider equality with God something to be used to his own advantage; rather, he made himself nothing by taking the very nature of a servant, being made in human likeness. **And being found in appearance as a man, he humbled himself by becoming obedient to death— even death on a cross!" Philippians 2:5-8 (NIV)**

Jesus lost more than just His arms and legs. He was obedient to death. And it wasn't just any death; it was the worst, most humiliating death of all. Jesus humbled Himself to lift you up.

As Nick says, there will be challenges in life. Everyone has them. But rather than giving up when things get tough, look to Jesus. He faced the worst things possible so that we too could be overcomers!

Not only does Jesus help you see the hurt in the world, but He gives you the ability to help.

Today, Nick speaks to others about Jesus. He may never be able to throw a football or jump rope, but he uses what God gave him to serve others. Your abilities will be different than Nick's. But each person can use their God-given gifts and talents to humble or lower themselves for others.

As Nick says, *"We can't, and we should not compare sufferings. We come together as a family of God, hand in hand. And then together coming and standing upon the promises of God, knowing that no matter who you are, no matter what you're going through, that God knows it, He is with you, He is going to pull you through."*

CHALLENGE: BE THANKFUL, BE CLEANSED

Choose to do one of these two options.

1. Nick was thankful for his voice and used it to spread the love of Jesus to others. Take time to thank God for your body.

2. Give something a bath today. Maybe your toys could use a good cleaning, or your puppy needs a scrub. Look at the dirty bathwater afterward. Think about how Jesus washed away our sins. Just like dirty water swirling down the drain, Jesus takes your sin away!

RED ALERT!

When the Bible talks about "Living Water," it means water that is moving, such as from a stream or spring. It is fresh and clean. If water isn't moving, it can become muddy and foul. In John 4, Jesus tells the woman at the well that He can give her Living Water, which will cleanse her and give her eternal life.

DAY 5

WHAT DID JESUS DO BY SERVING? (HE SAVED US!)

PANCAKE BALANCING ACT

Draw a giant stack of pancakes on the empty plate in the waiter's hand. How many of those pancakes do you think you can eat?

TAP THE SAP

It's breakfast time! Imagine you've got a tall stack of pancakes waiting for you at the kitchen table, smothered in butter. There's also a good chance you drizzled maple syrup on top.

Maple syrup comes from tree sap and is collected from maple trees in cold climates. When the air begins to warm in the spring, these trees shoot their sap back up through their bark to make new leaves. As the sap flows upward, people collect it by sinking short wooden straws—called "taps"—in the side of the tree.

After collecting a full bucket, the sap is boiled down, leaving the sugary sauce that we call maple syrup—a sweet part of breakfast!

As yummy as maple syrup might be, it's also mysterious. Scientists don't know what causes that rush of watery sap to shoot up to the very tips of the trees at the end of winter. Some people think it might be complicated processes with fancy names, like transpiration, capillary action, or osmosis. But those things do not explain everything.

Although no one really knows for sure how it works, this amazing event happens every spring—people tap the sap to create syrup.

BIG MYSTERIES

Sap is stored in a tree's roots under the ground to help the tree survive the bitter winter. But when warm weather arrives in the spring, that sap suddenly flows upward.

What does that remind you of?

This mystery reflects an even greater mystery. When Jesus died, He was buried in the ground. Like a tree in the dead of winter, all life seemed gone. But then came the springtime resurrection when Jesus rose up from the grave.

In other words…Life must go down and be buried before it can rise again.

THE SWEET SERVANT

Let's come back to the passage from Philippians for the grand finale. Here is the entire passage. Be sure to check out the paragraph in bold.

"In your relationships with one another, have the same mindset as Christ Jesus: Who, being in very nature God, did not consider equality with God something to be used to his own advantage; rather, he made himself nothing by taking the very nature of a servant, being made in human likeness. And being found in appearance as a man, he humbled himself by becoming obedient to death—even death on a cross!

"Therefore God exalted him to the highest place and gave him the name that is above every name, that at the name of Jesus every knee should bow, in heaven and on Earth and under the Earth, and every tongue acknowledge that Jesus Christ is Lord, to the glory of God the Father." Philippians 2:5-11 (NIV)

After Jesus died and all seemed lost, He rose to the highest place, higher than the tip-top of a maple tree. As a result, the Bible tells us, someday every knee will bow and every mouth will say that Jesus is Lord.

Jesus serves us so one day everyone will know that He is God. Jesus served us to save us. When we hear this good news, it bubbles up inside of us and we're inspired to serve one another. God is glorified through our serving. In other words, being a servant is sweet. It's sweeter than syrup.

CHALLENGE: LISTEN TO THE TREES

Serve your family by taking the dog for a walk or playing with your siblings at a park. While you do this, go on a nature walk and put your ear up to a tree trunk. Do you hear anything? If you live in a cold climate and it's spring, you may be able to hear the rushing of the tree sap in many (but not all) trees if it is very quiet. Better yet, use a stethoscope to listen to a tree. Write down what you hear.

RED ALERT!

The Bible often talks about "fruit" as the wonderful things in our lives. For example, Paul describes "spiritual fruit" in Galatians 5:22-23a: "But the fruit of the Spirit is love, joy, peace, forbearance, kindness, goodness, faithfulness, gentleness and self-control." So, be like trees and grow good fruit.

#SERVINGCHALLENGEKIDS

WHY DID SERVE?

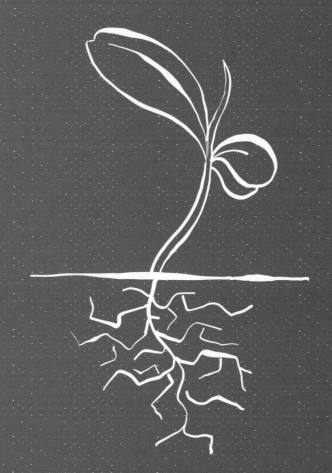

JESUS

THE FOREST OF REDVALE

PART 2

Aiden's stomach leaped when they made the jump from their living room to Redvale—all in the click of a TV remote. He was supposed to be at his basketball practice in one hour. Instead, he was a long, long way from home, surrounded by the trees of Redvale.

"Do you really need all three of us for this mission?" Aiden asked Red the Fox. "I have a basketball practice I can't miss."

The fox laughed. "The three of you come as a set. All for one and one for all!"

"Aiden, you need to slow down. Your sports schedule has been non-stop lately," came a familiar voice from behind. Aiden wheeled around to see Malachi hiking toward him, staff in hand.

Malachi, along with Red, had led them through three earlier adventures in Redvale. As usual, Malachi was dressed like a prophet of old, except for his gym shoes.

"But I don't have time for this," Aiden said.

"That's always your complaint," Emily griped.

Isabella didn't say a word. She kept clicking the TV remote, which she was still holding.

"You should know by now that electronic devices don't work in Redvale," Malachi said, gently lifting the remote from her hand.

"I can't miss basketball practice," Aiden insisted, looking around for a mysterious doorway leading back to their home in Florida. But all he saw were hundreds of trees in every direction.

"Do you even notice how bad the trees look?" Malachi asked.

"*I do!*" Emily exclaimed.

"I was asking Aiden." Malachi stroked his beard and waited for an answer.

Finally, Aiden took a good, hard look around. He *really* looked this time, and he realized Malachi was right. The trees were in awful shape. Most of their leaves were brown and shriveled, and their trunks were scarred by cracks and scratches. A strange growth clamped to the bark of many of them.

CRACK!

Hearing a loud snap, Aiden nearly jumped out of his shoes.

"Watch out!" Red hurled himself at Aiden, knocking him to the ground.

A maple tree crashed down, landing on the exact spot where Aiden had been standing only moments before. If the tree had landed on him, Aiden would've been flattened like a pancake (and topped with syrup from the maple tree).

"Stay alert," Malachi warned. "Trees are falling right and left."

Aiden's heart was still racing. "What's happening to them?"

"The Destroyers are attacking the Forest of Redvale on many fronts," said Red. "We need you to save them by serving them."

"I like that!" Emily exclaimed. "Saving by serving!"

"Can't it wait?" Aiden asked.

"Should Red have waited before he saved you from the falling tree?" Emily asked.

"Of course not! He had to act fast, or I would've been crushed."

Emily waved at a nearby tree. "It looks like these trees don't have a lot of time either."

A wild wind suddenly roared through the forest, turning one of the trees into a million particles of chaff. Aiden hated to admit it, but his sister had a point.

JESSE AND OLIVE

Emily hopped on top of a tree stump and glanced around at the dying forest. "How can we stop the Destroyers?"

"If you'll get off my head, I'll tell you."

Now, it was Emily's turn to nearly jump out of her shoes. The tree stump she stood upon had spoken!

Leaping off the stump, Emily blushed bright red. "I'm so sorry. I didn't realize…"

"How would you like it if I stood on your head without asking?" grumbled the tree stump, waving around its stick arms. The stump blinked its two large eyes with lids made of bark.

"Admit it, Jesse. You like to see people's shocked reactions when they stand or sit on you by mistake," came a woman's voice.

When Emily spun around, she spotted a tree walking toward them. Walking! The tree was not big, at least compared to most trees in the forest—only about twenty feet tall. This tree's eyes and mouth were near the top of the trunk, right below her crown of green leaves.

"Emily said she's sorry," the tree said to the stump. "You should forgive her, Jesse. It's a common mistake."

"Oh all right, I forgive you," growled the stump, but it was hard to tell if he meant it.

"So, your name is Jesse?" asked Isabella. She had been standing off to the side, pouting ever since they arrived in the forest. Emily could tell her sister was still mad about not having a working phone.

"Yes, and may I also introduce you to Olive," said Malachi, motioning toward the tree, who looked down at the kids and smiled.

"I suppose that means you're an olive tree," said Aiden.

The tree grinned. "How did you guess? But I bet you can't guess how old I am!"

Isabella folded her arms and frowned. "I thought it was impolite to guess someone's age."

"Not for trees. We're *proud* of our age!" said Olive. "Guess how old I am!"

"Just don't cut her down to count her annual rings," scowled Jesse. "I don't think she'd appreciate being turned into a stump like me."

Olive let loose with a big laugh. "Besides, olive trees are strange because we don't even have annual rings."

Emily didn't know if she should laugh along or not. She looked the olive tree up and down, from root to leaves, and took a wild guess. "Are you five hundred years old?"

Olive clapped her branches and grinned. "I'm one thousand four hundred and twenty-two years old!"

"Wow!" Emily exclaimed.

"And I'm part of the Netser family," Olive added. "You may have heard of us."

Emily had never heard of them, but she didn't want to admit it. She already felt stupid for standing on Jesse's head.

"Netser is a Hebrew word for 'shoot' or 'sprout,'" explained Red the Fox. "It's where we get the word for Nazareth."

"You mean the city where Jesus grew up?" asked Emily.

The olive tree reached out a branch and tapped Emily gently on the head—a motherly move. "That's right. Even today, you can find a lot of olive trees in Nazareth and the rest of Israel. We olive trees live long because we have strong roots."

"While that's all fine and good, I don't think we have time to talk about the history of olive trees," Malachi said, stepping forward. "I hate to interrupt, but we've got to save the forest!"

Jesse glared at Emily, looking her up and down. "This human seems kinda puny. Do you really think she can help us?"

Emily wanted to remind Jesse that she was taller than him, but she bit her lip. She put her hands on her hips and said, "What do we need to do?"

"The first thing is to get these acorns to a safe place—away from the clutches of the Seed Snatchers," said Malachi. He pointed to a large sack that hung from one of Olive's branches. Malachi reached into the sack and pulled out a handful of acorns.

"One of these acorns holds the life of a new oak tree," he said.

"What do you mean?" Aiden asked. "Won't every one of those acorns eventually become an oak tree?"

Malachi poured the acorns back in the sack. "I'm afraid not. If we're fortunate, one of those acorns will survive to become a tree."

"What about the rest?"

"They won't make it. Many will be devoured by animals."

"Or stolen by Seed Snatchers," said Olive. "The Snatchers won't rest until they steal every single one of these acorns."

"There are Givers in this world, and there are Takers," added Jesse. "The Seed Snatchers are Takers. They steal acorns and seeds and lock them up in a place where they can never grow—away from sunlight, water, and soil. I hate them!"

"Calm down, Jesse," said Olive gently, tapping him on his flat head.

"How do we know a Seed Snatcher when we see one?" Emily asked.

"Just look up," said Malachi. "But be very quiet. A Seed Snatcher is passing overhead right now."

A deep darkness came over them, a blanket of gloom. Emily looked up and shuddered. Through the tree canopy, she spotted the largest bird she ever saw. It glided above the treetops, with wings spread about twenty feet wide.

The bird was searching, peering through the trees. It was hunting.

SERVANTEERS AND SEED SNATCHERS

Isabella forgot all about not having a cell phone when she saw the gigantic bird flying above the trees.

They remained as quiet as possible as the shadow of the bird passed directly overhead, blocking the sun. The bird glided in circles for about five minutes before flapping its wings and disappearing into the distance.

Isabella let out a breath.

"We're okay. It's gone," said Malachi.

"A farmer went out to sow his seed. As he was scattering the seed, some fell along the path, and the birds came and ate it up," said Olive.

Isabella knew that Bible verse. It was from the Parable of the Sower. The seed was the Word of God, and the birds were the Evil Ones, devouring the words.

"Luke 8:5," said Isabella.

Olive grinned. "That's right. You know your Bible well."

Isabella stared at Olive in wonder. She had seen a lot of strange things in Redvale, but every time she encountered something new, she had a hard time believing her eyes and ears. A talking tree and tree stump? That was a new one.

"Our job is to protect the acorns from those monster birds," said Jesse, hopping up to Isabella. "It's just one of the jobs of the Servanteers."

"The who?"

"*The Servanteers!*" Jesse glanced at Malachi and said, "You mean these kids don't even know what a Servanteer is!"

Isabella blushed.

As Jesse mumbled grumpily, Olive explained. "Servanteers serve the trees of the forest by protecting their seeds and making sure they have enough water and sunlight. If you're willing, you can be Servanteers too."

"The Three Servanteers!" declared Red the Fox, jumping on top of Jesse's head.

"Off, off, off!" shouted Jesse, and the grinning fox obeyed.

Isabella didn't know anything about trees, so how could she serve them? Besides, it sounded like a lot of work.

"We'd love to be the Three Servanteers!" said Emily.

"Speak for yourself," said Isabella. "Maybe Aiden and I don't want to spend our time watering trees and carrying around a bag of acorns."

Even as she spoke, she was ashamed of her words. She tried not to look at Malachi.

"Isabella is right," said Aiden. "I have a big basketball game in a few days— and I need to learn some new plays. I don't have time to wander the forest."

Olive gave Isabella the saddest look she had ever seen on a tree. Granted, she had never seen a tree give her any kind of a look before.

"I'm sorry. It's just that—" Isabella stopped talking instantly, for she heard birds approaching. It sounded like the cawing of crows, only a hundred times louder.

"Hurry!" shouted Malachi. "We've been spotted!"

"Follow us!" said Olive, moving into action.

The cawing got louder and louder. Then they heard a crashing and crunching, and Isabella couldn't resist looking over her shoulder. Two enormous birds dove toward the ground, crashing through the branches, breaking them as easily as pretzels. The big birds were deep purple, with wild eyes and sharp, silver beaks.

"Run!" Malachi shouted. "I'll hold them off!"

Malachi turned to face the two birds, holding his staff above his head with both hands. The birds landed about fifteen feet away and eyed him cautiously.

Isabella felt Red tugging her hand. "C'mon! Stop gawking! Run!"

So, Isabella turned and took off, following Olive and Jesse deeper into the forest.

"Over here!" came a voice to their left.

Isabella turned toward the voice and spotted a stream. Lining the bank was a row of weeping willow trees with long, stringy branches that drooped to the ground. One of the trees motioned them over.

"We're sad to see you in trouble," blubbered the weeping willow, for it was crying. All the weeping willows were in tears.

"We'll hide you behind our branches," said another between sobs. "Oh, I'm so sad to see those mean birds after you." The tree blew his nose using an enormous handkerchief.

Isabella and the others followed Olive as she stepped through the curtain of drooping branches. By this time, all the willows were crying loudly, blowing their noses and moaning and wailing. It was very weird, but at least the drooping branches hid them from view.

"We can't let the Seed Snatchers steal our acorns," Olive said to Isabella, leaning over to whisper in her ear. "They're the only remaining acorns. If they're gone, all the oak trees in the forest will die."

"Quiet," hissed Jesse. "They're coming."

The two monster birds came into view. They hopped along the ground, looking down, as if searching for something.

Where was Malachi? Isabella wondered. She was afraid of what the birds might've done to him.

Suddenly, Malachi's voice sounded sharply from somewhere behind the two birds. It appeared that Malachi was trying to draw the birds away from the weeping willows.

Then Isabella felt an itch in her nose. She had bad allergies, and certain plants made her eyes water and her nose twitch. She squeezed her nose, trying to stifle the sneeze. Emily noticed and shook her head, as if to say, "No. Not now."

Isabella closed her eyes, concentrating all her power on stopping the sneeze. She thought she had won the battle when the sneeze snuck up on her and exploded before she had a chance to stop it.

"ACHOOOOOOO!"

The next instant, the birds were upon them—feathers and claws and silver-sharp beaks.

GIANT EARTHWORMS!

One of the big birds slammed into Aiden, sending him flying backward into the nearby stream. As he rose from the water, spluttering, he watched in horror as the Seed Snatchers lunged for the sack of acorns being carried by Olive.

The olive tree fought back bravely, using her many branches like hands, slapping at the birds as they went for the acorns.

Seconds later, Malachi was on the scene, using his staff in ways that Aiden had never seen before. Malachi tossed it on the ground, and the staff suddenly turned into a giant, juicy earthworm.

This caught the birds' attention. Both birds turned away from the acorns and went after the giant earthworm. The larger of the two birds gripped the worm by one end, while the other Seed Snatcher tugged on the opposite side.

Just as they began to devour the squirmy thing, the worm turned back into a wooden staff.

"COUGH! COUGH! GAG!"

The birds nearly choked on the staff.

While this was going on, Olive, Jesse, and the others made a run for it.

"Wait for me!" Aiden shouted, climbing the streambank and sprinting after them.

The two birds recovered quickly and were back in hot pursuit, flying just a few feet above the ground. One of the Seed Snatchers clamped down on the straps of the sack of acorns.

Olive held on with all her might, while Malachi tried to pry the bird's beak loose with his staff. But the bird was angry and determined.

CRACK!

One of Olive's branches, which held the sack of acorns, cracked in half, and the bird flew off with the sack of acorns in its beak. The other bird soon followed, but not before it gave Aiden another bump, sending him tumbling back into the stream.

THREE ACORNS

That night, as darkness set in, they gathered around a campfire. Malachi didn't want to burn ordinary wood because that might upset Olive and Jesse, who were made of wood, of course. So, he burned his staff instead!

Amazingly, the fire didn't destroy the staff. It burned without devouring the wood.

"I've never seen your staff do things like that," Emily said, staring into the fire.

"Yeah! Your staff turned into a giant worm! How cool!" said Aiden.

Malachi leaned forward, the glow of the fire dancing on his face. "There are many amazing things you have yet to see. The most incredible are still ahead of us."

"What happens now?" asked Isabella. "The birds took all of your acorns."

"Not all of them," said Red. "Each of you, check your pockets."

Emily dug a hand into her jean pocket and found a large acorn. "But how...?"

"I'm pretty good with tricks," said Red, holding up a coin—and making it disappear. "During the battle, I slipped an acorn into each of your pockets."

Aiden and Isabella also found an acorn in their pockets and drew them out.

"Those are the last three acorns," said Olive. "Guard them with your lives."

With our lives? Emily didn't like the sound of that.

"Remember, you're Servanteers now," added Jesse.

Malachi smiled. "Just like Jesus. He was the greatest of Servants."

"The Son of Man did not come to be served, but to serve," said Isabella. "Mark 10:45."

"But what good are three acorns?" Emily asked. "Don't you need hundreds of them? Like you said, you need lots of them in the hopes that a few will sprout and grow."

"That's true, but God still works, even when the odds are against Him," Malachi pointed out. "With God on our side and the right conditions, you need only one acorn to grow a tree."

Emily leaped to her feet. "So, let's plant them right here and now!"

Malachi put up a hand. "This isn't the right soil. We need to find the ideal location."

"And where's that?" asked Aiden.

"We can look for it tomorrow," said Olive. "Tonight, you need to rest."

"I could sleep like a log," said Red, curling up at the foot of a tree.

"I don't like that expression," grumbled Jesse.

As everyone prepared for sleep, the fire burning on Malachi's staff became dimmer and dimmer. Emily snuggled next to Red, who put his soft tail across her body like a blanket. As she drifted into sleep, she listened to the wind rustling through the trees.

Far in the distance, she heard a crack and crash. Another tree was falling to the ground. The sound was sad and scary—but not as scary as the noise that woke her later in the middle of the night.

Emily heard a roar, yanking her from a deep sleep.

She shot up, staring into the inky darkness, her heart racing. Isabella was also awake, sitting up and wide-eyed.

Surely, whatever made that sound *had* to be dangerous.

TO BE CONTINUED ON PAGE 87.

DAY 6

JESUS STARTED SMALL TO DO BIG THINGS

SPREADING SEEDS

Below are six different ways that plants spread their seeds. Try to match the six descriptions with the key words below.

Key words:

FLOATING

GRAVITY

EXPLODING

WIND

HOOKS

ANIMALS

1. Seeds might look like tasty treats, but they don't get digested. They pass through critters' bodies and are scattered. Some are also buried underground.

2. Seeds grow with air trapped inside so they can drift on the water and spread.

3. Seed pods suddenly burst open, throwing seeds all over the place!

4. Seeds are covered with these things, making it possible to catch a ride on fur or clothing, later dropping off and spreading.

5. Tiny, lightweight seeds blow away. Some even have special parachutes or wings to help them soar through the air.

6. Some heavy seeds simply fall off the plant to the ground.

STARTING SMALL

Different seeds travel in different ways, but they all have the same goal. They all hope to be planted in the soil, grow, and become a plant.

When we look at majestic, tall trees, it's hard to imagine that they first started out as tiny seeds. But that is the way of life. Things begin small, and they grow and grow.

It's also the way that God came to us.

When Jesus came to us to serve, He began as the tiniest, most insignificant living thing possible. Jesus did not float down to us like a seed. He was not pulled down to Earth by gravity or carried here on the wind. Jesus began life on Earth smaller than a seed. He came as a single cell in His mother's body.

A cell is the smallest thing that can live on its own. Yet, it is what makes up all living things. That tiny, single cell developed into a baby who grew into an adult man. What's more, Jesus wasn't born into a rich and famous family. He was born to a carpenter and his wife, and He grew up in an unimportant town called Nazareth.

People didn't think anyone important could come from little Nazareth. But God had a plan and a purpose. Here is what Jesus said about something small becoming something big.

> **"God's kingdom is like an acorn that a farmer plants. It is quite small as seeds go, but in the course of years it grows into a huge oak tree, and eagles build nests in it." Matthew 13:31-32 (MSG)**

From small things come great things. Jesus is our King, but He is a King like no other. He is a King who serves us—and He calls us to be servants as well.

SERVANT SAMPLES

Just as seeds come in different shapes and sizes and spread in different ways, there are many different types of servants and ways to serve. The Bible talks about many servants, and each one is unique. Here are just two examples:

- **Mary.** When Jesus's mother, Mary, was told by the angel that she would become pregnant with the Son of God, she described herself as a servant.

  "And Mary said, 'Behold, I am the servant of the Lord; let it be to me according to your word.' And the angel departed from her." Luke 1:38 (ESV)

- **Paul.** The apostle Paul said he is a slave to everyone, even non-Christians.

  "Though I am free and belong to no one, I have made myself a slave to everyone, to win as many as possible." 1 Corinthians 9:19 (NIV)

Being a servant in this world may seem like an impossible job. But even if something is small, it is still powerful. Seeds teach us that. For example, one orchid seed pod holds up to three million seeds! And if you drive through an enormous forest, just remember: All of those trees began as seeds.

So, small things can do big things. A kid can change the world. God will make possible what seems impossible!

  "The simple truth is that if you had a mere kernel of faith, a poppy seed, say, you would tell this mountain, 'Move!' and it would move. There is nothing you wouldn't be able to tackle." Matthew 17:20b (MSG)

CHALLENGE: SMALL IS BEAUTIFUL

What might be keeping you from being a servant? Circle them below and/or add your own.

- I am small.
- I am young.
- I am quiet.
- I am shy.
- I am not smart.
- I can't read.
- I don't have friends.
- I don't understand Jesus.

- I have doubts.
- I don't like to talk to strangers.
- I get tired easily.
- I just like to stay home.
- I am not athletic.
- I don't like to clean.
- I don't like to volunteer.
- _____

God can take what you think is a negative and turn it into a positive. He can take what you think is wrong with you and use it to change the world.

RED ALERT!

Jesus liked to pray at the Mount of Olives—a hill just east of Jerusalem with lots of olive trees. Luke 22:39 says Jesus went there "as usual," so it must've been a regular spot for Him. The Garden of Gethsemane is at the base of the Mount of Olives.

DAY 7

JESUS KNEW WHO HE WAS AND HELPS US KNOW WHO WE ARE TOO

DIGGING DEEP

When a seed is planted in the soil and receives water and sunlight, it begins to grow. Do you think it grows the roots or the leaves first?

Write your answer here:

If you said "roots," you are correct!

When a plant grows, the first thing we see, sticking out of the ground, is a tiny shoot with leaves. But before that shoot appeared, the plant was busily growing roots in the ground. God designed roots to grow deep in the dark soil, where the plant will get its water, nutrients (food), and strength. Even though we can't see roots, they are just as important as the leaves. They also keep the plant firmly in one place, so it can grow.

THE ROOT OF JESSE

Long before Jesus was born, the prophet Isaiah talked about the "root of Jesse." Isaiah said that all nations will "rally to him." (Isaiah 11:1-10) People believe the root of Jesse is talking about the Messiah—Jesus. After all, Jesus was related to Jesse, the father of King David. In other words, in the Old Testament, long before we saw Jesus, God was putting down roots. He was planting the seeds of His Kingdom. He knew that Jesus, a descendant of Jesse, would come to save the world.

Jesus served because He knew His roots. He knew that the Kingdom of Heaven was His home and that He was God.

> **"Jesus answered,** 'I am the way and the truth and the life. No one comes to the Father except through me.'" **John 14:6 (NIV)**

THE THREE IN ONE

Jesus understands who He is. He knows He is one part of a "Triune" God. But this is not an easy idea to understand. "Trinity" is the word we use to describe God's three parts, united into one:

- God the Father
- God the Son
- God the Holy Spirit

All three parts of God are equal, and one wasn't created before the others. All three persons have always existed, loving and serving each other. Although this can be confusing, stories in the Bible help us see the three parts of God. One of those stories was Jesus's baptism.

THE HOLY BAPTISM

When Jesus was baptized, all three parts of God were present. Read the verses below. Can you spot the three parts of God?

> **"And when Jesus was baptized, immediately he went up from the water, and behold, the heavens were opened to him, and he saw the Spirit of God descending like a dove and coming to rest on him; and behold, a voice from heaven said, 'This is my beloved Son, with whom I am well pleased.'" Matthew 3:16-17 (ESV)**

Match the words on the right with the persons of the Trinity to the left.

GOD THE FATHER   DOVE

GOD THE SON   VOICE

GOD THE HOLY SPIRIT   JESUS

Next, look up Matthew 28:19 in your Bible. Then fill in the blanks with the three names in which we are baptized.

Therefore go and make disciples of all nations,
baptizing them in the name of the _____
and of the _____
and of the _____ .
Matthew 28:19 (NIV)

WE ARE MADE TO SERVE

Jesus knew His identity. He knew who He was and what He needed to do on earth. He came to serve us and save us. God gives you an identity too. And if you know who you are in God, you know your purpose in life:

● God created us to serve! It's what we NEED to do!

● We are God's children. We belong to Jesus.

● God saved us from our sins. Our serving doesn't save us—God does. We don't serve to earn brownie points.

● Because Jesus rose again, we have a chance to bring God's Kingdom to earth. Serving is one way we can show Jesus to other people.

CHALLENGE: EXPLORE YOUR ROOTS

People use the word "roots" when talking about where they are from. Fill in the blanks below, which describe your roots. Then think of someone you are connected to through your roots. Find a way to serve that person in the next week.

MY ROOTS

My name is _____.

I am _____ years old.

I was born in _____ on _____.

I live in _____ with _____.

My parents are _____.

I go to _____ school and attend _____church.

Some of the people I'm related to are:

_____

_____

_____

_____

_____

_____

DAY 8

JESUS SERVED BY BEING PATIENT

SLOW AND STEADY

Trees do not grow quickly.

It takes humans around eighteen years to grow from a baby to a full-grown adult. It can take a tree 100 years to reach its full height. That's about five times longer than humans grow.

When we think about growing up, it can seem forever. Eighteen years seems like a long time to grow. It's tempting to want to skip over the boring stuff during those years, but beware of what you wish for. A French fable shows us that it might not be a good idea. Check out this story, "The Magic Thread," adapted from William J. Bennett's *The Book of Virtues*.

THE GOLDEN THREAD

There once was a boy named Peter who was always waiting for the next thing to happen. He was never happy where he was. One day, he met an old woman. She offered him a silver ball with a small golden thread hanging from the end.

"This is your timeline thread," she explained. Whenever he wanted to make time pass quickly, he simply pulled the thread. If he was bored at school, a tiny yank would skip him to the end of the day.

"But once the thread has been pulled, it can't be put back," the old woman warned.

Peter decided to give it a try. The next day, his math teacher almost put him to sleep with a boring lesson. So, he gave the string a little tug. Suddenly, it was the end of the day, and he heard the bell ringing. Peter gave a whoop and ran out the door. This was the best day of his life!

For the rest of the week, Peter pulled the string as soon as he got bored. Then **ZAP!** He was at the end of the day.

Each year, Peter pulled on the string more and more until before he knew it, he was an old man and found himself doing nothing but watching TV or sleeping.

Finally, one day he went on a slow walk. In his pocket, the silver ball was now the size of a tiny marble. There was not much left. He pulled out his silver ball and looked at the string all piled up next to it.

"I wish I could go back and live my life again," he said to himself. "I would do things so differently."

At that moment, the same old woman appeared again. "Peter, how was your life?" she asked.

"I don't really know," he said. "I skipped over most of it. All I have left to show is this bundle of gold thread. It doesn't do me much good. I don't have any memories. I'd love a second chance to relive my life without the magic ball."

The wise woman nodded silently and smiled. "Your wish is granted."

In an instant, Peter found himself back in the woods as a child again. The silver ball was gone, but he was okay with that.

"I'm ready to live my life again, boring parts and all!" Then Peter ran off with a skip in his stride.

GROWING UP

In the Bible, four men wrote about Jesus's life in books called Matthew, Mark, Luke, and John. Almost all the stories from those books talk about Jesus when He was the ages thirty to thirty-three. But that's only three years of Jesus's life!

What happened during all the other years?

During the other thirty years of Jesus's life, He was preparing. Like Peter in "The Magic Thread," Jesus had the ability to make the time go by quickly. But He did not give in to the temptation. Jesus waited patiently until it was the right time to begin His work.

This is what the Bible says about Jesus growing up. **"And Jesus grew in wisdom and stature, and in favor with God and man." Luke 2:52 (NIV)**

For the first thirty years of His life, Jesus prepared for His ministry of serving.

Even though there are boring parts to life, those might be the times that God has given you to get ready to serve. Besides, no matter how little you are, you can still serve others now.

So, let's be patient as we learn what it means to serve. Don't skip the boring parts. Those might just be the most important parts of all!

CHALLENGE: STAGES OF GROWTH

Below is a picture of a growing seed. If serving others was a seed, which stage do you think you are in? Mark your stage below.

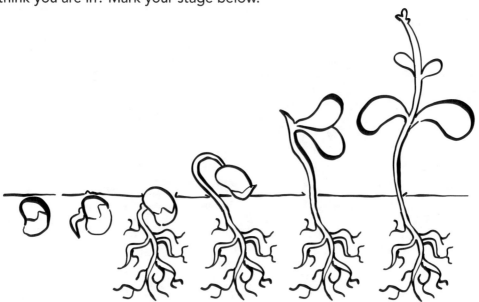

_____ Stage 1—I am just starting out. I don't know what I am supposed to do.

_____ Stage 2—I have a little shoot coming out, but I'm still figuring it out.

_____ Stage 3—I have a root. I serve a little.

_____ Stage 4—I am not shy. I'm ready to come out of hiding to meet others.

_____ Stage 5—I am excited to keep growing, and I'm taking steps in my faith so I can serve more.

_____ Stage 6—I am strong in my serving. I know what Jesus needs me to do, and I am excited to keep learning.

No matter what stage you are in, you can still serve others. Help someone out today, even if you don't feel like you are a spectacular servant.

DAY 9

JESUS SHOWED UP EVEN WHEN THE ODDS WERE AGAINST HIM

NUTS!

Trees make millions and even billions of seeds in their lifetime. But very few of all those seeds ever grow into a fully mature tree. For example, a beech tree will make 1.8 million beech nuts in its lifetime. But out of all those nuts, only one will grow into a full-grown tree. One out of 1.8 million!

For a poplar tree, the odds are even worse. Only one of its 1.1 billion seeds will turn into a full-grown tree. So, while the odds of turning into a full-grown tree might be slim, each seed still gets dropped from the tree. Every seed hopes to become a tree.

When Jesus came into the world, His odds of succeeding were not much better than those acorns. King Herod tried to wipe out Jesus by killing every baby boy under age two in and around Bethlehem. So, already the odds of Jesus surviving were almost zero percent. But God made a way. He sent Mary and Joseph fleeing to Egypt, and Jesus escaped the sword.

Even when the odds were stacked against Him, Jesus still came to save us and serve us. Here are three ways Jesus showed He was there to help.

① HE SAID IT!
"Repent, for the kingdom of heaven has come near." **Matthew 4:17b (NIV)**

Jesus said the Kingdom of Heaven "has come near," but where exactly is it? What does that mean?

The Kingdom of Heaven is anywhere that God rules. Jesus's good news is that there is hope for everyone to live in peace with God in His Kingdom.

② HE MADE TIME!
"Jesus went throughout Galilee, teaching in their synagogues, proclaiming the good news of the kingdom..." Matthew 4:23a (NIV)

Jesus walked all around Galilee in the northern part of Israel, which was His home where He grew up. Galilee was 13 miles long and 8.1 miles wide. That's a lot of steps! But Jesus took the time and went to the places closest to Him.

③ HE SHOWED IT!
"...and healing every disease and sickness among the people. News about him spread all over Syria, and people brought to him all who were ill with various diseases, those suffering severe pain, the demon-possessed, those having seizures, and the paralyzed; and he healed them." Matthew 4: 23b-24 (NIV)

The Bible says Jesus felt sorry for people and helped many of them. He showed His love. There were over 100 small towns in Galilee in Jesus's time, and He visited many of them, telling people the good news.

In addition to preaching, Jesus performed many miracles. Circle all the miracles you see in the verses from Matthew 4 on the previous page.

Even though it may have seemed like an impossible task, Jesus came to serve you.

● He says He loves you.

● He makes time for you.

● He shows His love. He takes care of you every day.

Jesus wants you to follow His example. You don't need to worry about how you will do it or if you will fail. When the odds seem against you, trust that God is on your side. He has a plan. So, if you are ready to serve using God's strength, how can you show His love to people?

1 **YOU CAN SAY IT!**
Tell someone you want to serve them. Often, we assume people can read our minds. We think they know we want to serve, so we wait for them to ask. But no one knows that you want to serve unless you tell them.

2 **YOU CAN MAKE THE TIME!**
Write down the name of your city/town and its population.

City/Town: _____

Population: _____

In Jesus's time, roughly three million people lived in Galilee. We don't know how many of them Jesus healed, but He didn't make it hard to find Him as He walked around, speaking about the Kingdom of Heaven.

We too don't need to make it hard for others to find us! You can serve the people in your home, school, church, team, or neighborhood.

③ YOU CAN SHOW IT!

It can be overwhelming when you think about serving everyone. So, start small. When you help just one person, you show what God's love looks like.

It might seem sad that not every seed will become a tree. But every seed still serves a purpose. Some become food. Others turn back into dirt, putting rich nutrients back in the ground, which will then be ready to be used by plants. It's the same when you scatter the seeds of God's Word. You never know what those words are doing in the hearts of others.

Not all of your serving will create big changes, but every time you serve, it is used by God. That's a 100-percent guarantee!

CHALLENGE: NUTS!

Help Mr. Squirrel by circling all the nuts you can find in the picture. Then, make a treat basket filled with snacks and water for your local mail or delivery person. Leave it on the front porch along with a card on which you write the words of **Deuteronomy 31:8**.

DAY 10
JESUS GAVE US INSTRUCTIONS FOR PLANTING THE WORD

THE BIG THREE

Good things (like the Trinity) come in threes. All plants need the same three basic things:

SUN • **WATER** • **DIRT (SOIL)**

However, the type of soil and the amount of sun and water needed is different for each plant. In addition, you need to think about many other things, such as differences in fertilizer (plant food), pruning (trimming), temperature, amount of care, and whether a plant is pet-friendly. If your seed is not growing properly, there's a good chance that one of these things may need to be changed.

Guidebooks will explain such differences with symbols like these:

PLANTS CAN TOLERATE INTENSE SUNLIGHT.   **PLANTS THRIVE WITH INDIRECT SUNLIGHT.**   **PLANTS CAN GROW IN SHADE.**

PLANTS MUST BE WATERED OFTEN.

PLANTS CAN GET BY WITH INFREQUENT WATERING.

PLANTS CAN TOLERATE DRY PERIODS.

PLANTS DO FINE IN HIGH TEMPERATURES.

PLANTS DO BEST IN MEDIUM TEMPERATURES.

PLANTS CAN SURVIVE COLD.

THE GREAT MISSION

Planting the seeds of the Word of God also calls for the same kind of care. That's why Jesus gave us many instructions on how to grow the Kingdom and plant the seeds of the Good Word.

One of His most famous set of instructions came in what is called the Great Commission.

If you're wondering what "commission" means, think of it as the Great Mission. Jesus sent His disciples on a Great Mission in this passage from Matthew:

"'God authorized and commanded me to commission you: Go out and train everyone you meet, far and near, in this way of life, marking them by baptism in the threefold name: Father, Son, and Holy Spirit. Then instruct them in the practice of all I have commanded you. I'll be with you as you do this, day after day after day, right up to the end of the age.'" **Matthew 28:18b-20 (MSG)**

Before Jesus gave the disciples the Great Commission, He sent them on short trips to preach to the people of Israel. Jesus made sure that they were prepared and, most importantly, He promised to be with them.

If the Great Commission were printed as a set of guidelines, like instructions on a packet of seeds, it might look something like this:

PLANTING THE WORD OF GOD

WHAT YOU'LL NEED:

1 **THE SON'S LIGHT**

Give people plenty of the Son's light. The light of Jesus will show the Way to God. It will give people joy and purpose to their life.

2 **LIVING WATER**

Jesus called himself Living Water, which is water that cleanses. Jesus cleans us of our sins. So, be sure to use plenty of Living Water. It will wash away all of your guilt.

3 **AN OPEN HEART**

Like seeds in a good soil, the Word of God grows best in an open heart. The Word will grow and flourish.

Once you have these three things, follow the steps below:

- Go to all the nations.
- Baptize.
- Teach people to obey.
- Jesus will be with us always!

The Great Commission wasn't only for Jesus's disciples. It's for you as well because Jesus is sending all of us on a Great Mission. You aren't delicate or breakable. God made you brave and strong. So, go into your school, be involved in activities, and build friendships. Show people what the Kingdom of God looks like.

Plant some seeds today!

CHALLENGE: COMPASSION COUPONS

Let others know the ways you can serve. For instance, make a coupon book to share with someone. Find a coupon book to print and fill in by going to our website WWW.SERVINGCHALLENGE.COM/FREE-KIDS-RESOURCES.

Perhaps you really like giving hugs, or you're a great artist and would love to color a picture for someone. Maybe you would prefer doing a chore for someone. Cut out your coupons and hand them to different people or make a coupon book for only one person. Then get ready to serve!

DAY 11

JESUS GAVE EVERYTHING

CALIFORNIA DREAMIN'

When we serve, we give up something so someone else can receive. Jesus gave up His life so we could receive eternal life. In California, a man named César Chávez suffered. He gave up his comfort so others could receive a better life.

When César was a young boy, his family lost their farm because of the Great Depression and moved to California to become migrant workers. César picked beans, cherries, and lettuce in the spring; grapes, tomatoes, and corn in the summer; and cotton in the fall.

Because his family moved around so much, César attended sixty-five schools. That is more than five moves each year! At age fifteen, he quit school to take care of his family because his father got hurt. When César grew up, he remembered how unfairly farmworkers were treated.

Even though César was shy, he began to speak out and urged other poor farmers to vote. He also fought to make sure they were treated better. Grape pickers earned only one dollar per hour. César started the United Farm Workers Organizing Committee (UFWOC) and made the drastic choice to **not eat** until farmers treated their workers better.

It worked! Farmers began to pay their workers more money. Senator Robert F. Kennedy flew across the country to give César his first piece of bread to break his fast!

Later, César fasted again to help improve the chemicals sprayed on the plants to keep the workers from getting sick. When César died, President Bill Clinton gave his wife the Presidential Medal of Freedom.

BECOMING A SERVANT

César wanted to serve the migrant workers of California because he knew what life was like for them. Instead of getting angry at the farmers, he decided to get their attention and work his entire life to make sure others were treated better than he was. César Chavez served others his entire life. He said, *"Being of service is not enough. You must become a servant of the people."*

César knew there was a difference between serving every once in a while and **being** a servant. A servant is always giving and helping. Jesus was the best example of a servant.

César loved and believed in God. Knowing that Jesus suffered for him helped him to be willing to suffer for others. As Mark 10:45 (NIV) says, **"For even the Son of Man did not come to be served but to serve and to give his life as a ransom for many."**

FOOD, FASTING, AND FAITH

César fasted to protest the terrible work conditions of farm workers. He gave up eating until the workers were treated better.

In the Bible, Jesus regularly fasted too, but not as a protest. It was a way to connect with God. For example, Jesus fasted for forty days in the wilderness! Forty days without food is mind boggling.

Jesus knew that before He served others, it was important to spend time with God. So, He did that by fasting and praying in the wilderness. (To dig deeper into how you can do this, check out *Being Challenge Kids*.)

Fasting, or giving up food, is one way to connect with God. Food also helps us connect with others. However, in this case, we're not giving up food. We're *sharing* meals with people! Sharing a meal is one way people tell others they care about them. Jesus showed sinners He cared about them by eating with them—something that got people pretty angry, as you can see in the story of Zacchaeus in Luke 19:1-10.

One day, Jesus saw a man named Zacchaeus climbing a tree. Zacchaeus was a small guy and couldn't see Jesus above the crowd, so he climbed a tree to get a better view. Jesus called to him, **"Zacchaeus, you come down. I am going to your house today!"**

Boy, were people mad! Nobody liked tax collectors because they were liars and cheats. And Zacchaeus was the "chief tax collector." He was the Boss Tax Man. But that didn't stop Jesus from eating with him.

THE LAST SUPPER

Eating with people and fasting were only the first steps on the long road to Calvary, where Jesus died on the cross. Jesus was killed on Golgotha, the "place of the skull" as it was known.

Before He died, Jesus spent one last meal with his followers, the disciples. This was called the Last Supper, and we celebrate it every time we take Communion. At Communion, we celebrate that Christ became the greatest servant by dying for us.

We can be grateful for people like César Chavez who gave his life in service to others. But César knew he could not serve all on his own. He needed God's strength. You too need God's power.

When you serve, God will help you and give you the strength that you need. Count on it.

CHALLENGE: SHARE A MEAL

César Chávez once said, *"If you really want to make a friend, go to someone's house and eat with him...the people who give you their food give you their heart."*

Your challenge today is to share food with another person at home. Eating with others is a way to serve others.

RED ALERT!

Philippians 2:5-11 is called "The Christ Hymn." The early church in the first century often recited these verses, which taught that Jesus came to SERVE. The way He served us was by dying on the cross.

DAY 12

JESUS SERVED US BECAUSE HE LOVES US

IN REVIEW...

So far, you have learned that:

1. Jesus came down to Earth as a human, beginning as a teeny tiny cell.

2. Jesus knew He was the Son of God. He knew His purpose on earth.

3. Jesus took His time, growing up just like you.

4. Jesus knew when He was ready to help the people He would serve.

5. Jesus provided clear instructions on how to serve.

6. Jesus gave up everything for us, even His life. He not only died but was separated from God.

Today, we're going to learn about the greatest reason why Jesus serves us— LOVE.

TREE CONNECTIONS

Far away in Africa, scientists watched a herd of giraffes settle in for lunch. The giraffes gobbled leaves from a group of umbrella thorn acacia trees. But when the acacia trees sensed the animals were eating their leaves, they sounded an alert.

Danger! Danger! The acacia trees started pumping bitter poison into their leaves, so the giraffes would stop munching on them.

When their lunch turned sour, the giraffes moved on to other trees. But what surprised the scientists was that the giraffes moved over 100 yards away, the distance of a football field. They discovered that the trees being eaten had sounded the alarm for their neighbors, forcing the giraffes to move far away.

The trees sent special "scent messages" to the nearby acacias. When the other trees detected the danger alarm, they too began pumping bitter poison into their leaves, even though they hadn't yet been munched on. Through odor, trees "talked" to one another.

This kind of thing doesn't just happen in Africa. All over the world, trees in forests send signals to one another.

- Oaks change their leaves so much that they become terribly bitter, and they warn their neighbors to do the same. Yuck!

- Willow trees also give off smells. They have specific scents to drive away certain insects, so their neighbors know exactly what's coming. Pee-ew!

- Trees use their underground network of fungi to send electric signals to each other like an underground Morse Code!

- Researchers discovered that young corn roots "crackle" at a frequency of 220 hertz. Tiny seedling plants move their root tips in the direction of the crackling. This means some plants even communicate through sound waves.

Scientists are still discovering the different ways trees and plants send signals to each other. The trees may not speak with mouths, but it's a scientific fact that trees communicate with each other—and the reason they do it is the same. They "talk" to help one another.

CHRISTIAN CONNECTIONS

Just as trees are connected to one another, so are followers of Jesus. We may be male and female, have different color skin, have different interests and talents, have different strengths and weaknesses, but we're still linked in the most important way possible—through Jesus. He unites us all in LOVE.

Jesus is also the reason we serve each other. As it says in 1 John 3:16-17, **"This is how we know what love is: Jesus Christ laid down his life for us. And we ought to lay down our lives for our brothers and sisters. If anyone has material possessions and sees a brother or sister in need but has no pity on them, how can the love of God be in that person?" (NIV)**

There are many different reasons why people serve each other.

- Some serve because it is their job.

- Some serve because they are parents or guardians. They serve their families.

- Some serve because it feels good to help others.

- Some serve because they want someone to have a better life.

These are all great reasons to serve. We are thankful for people like police officers and firemen because they keep us safe. And serving does feel good.

But there's another reason for serving…

POWERFUL LOVE

Jesus asks us to serve. When you see others and want to help, you're looking at others the way that Jesus does—with the eyes of LOVE.

Jesus serves us because He LOVES us, and He wants us to serve others with the same kind of powerful love. Jesus loves us so much that He died on the cross for us. But His story didn't end at the cross. Read in Mark about what happened to Jesus after He died.

> **"Very early on the first day of the week, they were on their way to the tomb. It was just after sunrise. They asked each other, 'Who will roll the stone away from the entrance to the tomb?'**
>
> **"Then they looked up and saw that the stone had been rolled away. The stone was very large. They entered the tomb. As they did, they saw a young man dressed in a white robe. He was sitting on the right side. They were alarmed.**
>
> **"'Don't be alarmed,' he said. 'You are looking for Jesus the Nazarene, who was crucified. But he has risen! He is not here! See the place where they had put him. Go! Tell his disciples and Peter, "He is going ahead of you into Galilee. There you will see him. It will be just as he told you."'" Mark 16:2-7 (NIRV)**

When Jesus died, some crazy things happened. The sky grew dark for three hours in the middle of the day. A widespread earthquake shook the land. Perhaps this reminded people of all the things that happened when God gave Moses the Ten Commandments.

After Jesus died, He was buried, like a seed in the ground. As the Bible says in John 12:24 of *The Message*, **"Listen carefully: Unless a grain of wheat is buried in the ground, dead to the world, it is never any more than a grain of wheat. But if it is buried, it sprouts and reproduces itself many times over."**

A seed must be buried before it can explode from the ground with new life—and it was the same with Jesus. When He rose from the dead, when He rose from the ground, it was like a beautiful plant, growing and producing fruit. It's also the same for us. We must die before we can rise to eternal life.

After the disciples learned that Jesus had risen from the grave, the news spread like crazy. Just as trees communicate, sending signals through fungi underground and smells in the air, the Good News about Jesus spread through the connections among Christians.

The world was never the same again.

So, spread the Word and spread His LOVE. Tell people that Jesus died to give them life eternal. He defeated death!

But as you spread the Word, don't forget to serve. Serving isn't something you have to do. It's something you get to do! LOVE and serving are linked. And if trees can help each other, so can we.

CHALLENGE: HELPING IN A DISASTER

Help someone who has lived through a natural disaster today. Start by praying for them. Ask your parents to help you research some of the latest natural disasters in your city, state, country, or even world. How can you serve those people today?

RED ALERT!

Scientists found evidence of an earthquake in the area around Jerusalem between 26 and 36 AD. This is close to the time that Jesus would have died. Maybe it was the earthquake that occurred when He was killed on the cross.

#SERVINGCHALLENGEKIDS

WHEN D
JESUS

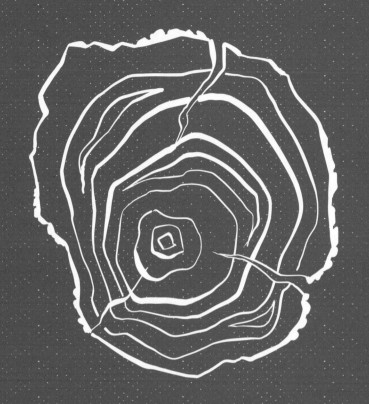

D

SERVE?

THE FOREST OF REDVALE

PART 3

During the long, dark night, Isabella heard a ferocious growl, echoing through the forest. Sitting up, she noticed that Emily had also been awakened by the roar.

"What is *that*?" Isabella whispered.

Emily shrugged. "I don't think I want to know."

It took Isabella forever to fall back asleep. And when she finally did, she continued to hear the growl in her dreams. Come morning, as the group prepared to venture deeper into the forest, Isabella brought her fears into the open. "What was that terrible sound?"

"I was wondering when you were going to ask," Malachi said, drawing in the dirt with his staff.

"It's the Humongous Fungus," said Olive, shaking her leaves and stretching her branches as she slowly woke up. (Yes, the trees in Redvale sleep too.)

"Humongous Fungus? Is the creature as bad as it sounds?" Isabella asked.

"Worse," said Jesse.

Olive cut a sideways glance at Jesse. "No need to scare her."

"But she needs to know the truth. The Humongous Fungus is the forest's biggest bully."

"That's right," said Red. The little fox had a small stick in his hands and was using it to tickle the nose of Aiden, who was still asleep. "Like all bullies, the Humongous Fungus looks for weaknesses—cracks in the bark. Then it ATTACKS."

Malachi nodded. "And that's why we need to stop him."

Isabella's heart skipped a beat. "Stop him? I thought our mission was to find the right soil to plant our acorns." She patted her pocket, where she carried one of the three remaining acorns.

"It is," said Malachi. "But if we follow the WAY, our path will take us right past the lair of the Humongous Fungus. We must march through it."

"That's how it is with most hard things in life," said Olive. "You can't run away from them. You must face them directly."

Isabella thought about their last adventure in Redvale, when they tangled with two bullies. "You're right. We stood up to Frankie and Chloe, and now they're great friends."

"But you didn't just stand up to Frankie and Chloe," said Malachi. "You risked your lives to save them. And there's no greater way of serving than that."

"No one has greater love than the one who gives their life for their friends," said Isabella, quoting John 15:13.

"Amen!" exclaimed Aiden, suddenly waking up. Red's non-stop tickling finally did the trick.

"Now that Aiden is awake, we better get moving," said Jesse. "It's better to face the Humongous Fungus early in the morning, before he's had his coffee."

Aiden glanced at Emily and Isabella, his eyes wide. "Humongous Fungus? What did I miss?"

"Jesse is right," said Malachi, rising to his feet. "No time to lose. We'll explain on the way, Aiden."

THE OIL PRESS

The more Malachi talked about the Humongous Fungus, the more nervous Aiden became. His legs were telling him to turn around and run in the opposite direction. And if he was completely honest, so were his arms, ears, nose, and eyes. Every part of his body tingled with terror.

"There must be an easier way to plant these acorns than to face this creature," he said.

"Believe me, there isn't," said Olive.

"And an olive tree should know something about facing trials," said Red. "Did you know that olive trees were with Jesus in the Garden of Gethsemane, the night before He died on the cross? In the Garden, Jesus knew He couldn't run away from His death. He had to face it head on."

"That's what Servanteers do," added Olive. "They serve, even when things are really hard."

"Also, the word 'Gethsemane' means 'oil press!'" Red added as they hiked uphill, with trees leaning in from all sides. "There was an oil press near the Garden where Jesus prayed."

"What's an oil press for?" Aiden asked. "Is it for making motor oil?"

As Red tumbled on the ground laughing, Aiden turned as red as...well, as red as Red. When Malachi scolded Red with a look, the fox stopped laughing and said, "Sorry."

"An oil press is for making olive oil, not motor oil, silly," said Jesse. "It uses a huge stone to crush olives, squeezing oil out of them."

"People in Jesus's day used the oil for cooking and lamps," Red added.

"When you press olives, you crush them *three* times," added Malachi. "During Bible days, the first crushing created the best oil, which was used by the priests in the Temple. The second crushing created oil for medicine, cosmetics, and food. Then the third crushing made oil used in lamps."

Red the Fox started hopping around and waving his hand. "Ooh, ooh, ooh, let me tell the next part! It's really amazing!"

Malachi sent him a gentle smile. "You may, Red."

Red jumped on top of Jesse the stump, who frowned and muttered to himself.

"In the Garden of Gethsemane, Jesus prayed *three times*—just like olives are crushed *three* times!" Red declared. "Each time Jesus prayed, it felt like He was being crushed by the weight of our sins, like the rock crushing the olives. He even sweated blood, like the last drops of oil being squeezed from the olives!"

Aiden shook his head in wonderment. He was never going to look at olives— or what happened in the Garden of Gethsemane—the same way again.

"Olive trees are amazing," Aiden said.

"I know," said Jesse. "We *are* amazing!"

"Wait…Are you an olive tree too?" asked Emily.

Jesse frowned and grumbled. "Of course I am. You mean you can't tell?"

"You should've seen Jesse in his prime before he was cut down," Olive said. "He was quite a handsome olive tree!"

That seemed to soothe the irritable stump.

"But enough about olive trees," Malachi said. "We've got a mission before us." He pointed his staff toward a narrow path, winding through the forest. "This is the WAY. It will take us to the ideal soil for planting our acorns."

Aiden sighed. This was also the path that will take them right past the Humongous Fungus. He thought about asking what the Fungus looked like, but he decided he'd rather not talk about it—or even think about it.

He had a feeling the creature would be even more terrible than he imagined.

HEARTWOOD

It didn't take a forester to see that the trees were sick. Almost every tree they passed had huge cracks in their sides. Many of them had already fallen, and some swayed and creaked in the wind. A couple of them turned into chaff right in front of their eyes and blew away in the wind.

"Be alert for falling trees," said Jesse. "If one fell on top of me, I'd be all right. But if one fell on your heads, you'd be goners."

Emily looked around at the trees, wondering which one would be the next to fall. She was nervous, but she trusted Malachi to protect them. He hadn't let them down…yet. She decided she would serve the forest any way she could. She was a Servanteer, after all! She liked the sound of the word.

"Thanks for going on this mission," Emily said, slipping beside Isabella. "I know the last thing you wanted was to leave your comfortable couch to sleep in a forest and battle giant birds and a Humongous Fungus."

"Did I really have a choice?" Isabella grumbled.

"We *all* have a choice," said Olive, coming up from behind. "Sorry, I couldn't help but overhear."

Isabella looked over her shoulder at the olive tree. "But I *didn't* have a choice. I clicked the TV remote, and the next second we were here in Redvale."

"But you can still go home, if you want," said Olive.

"I can?"

"Absolutely. Just ask Malachi, and he'll find a way to get you back home."

"Why did you have to tell her that?" Emily growled.

"Because it's true," said Olive. "We don't ever want to force someone to be a Servanteer. Serving has got to come from the heartwood."

"The what?"

"Heartwood is the strong, inner part of a tree," she said. "Serving takes strength—and it also makes you stronger. Every time a tree serves, its heartwood becomes stronger and firmer. But serving must be a choice. If you're forced to do it, that makes you a slave, not a servant."

"But Isabella needs to be pestered to get off the couch," Emily said.

"And it's your job to pester her?" asked Olive.

"She seems to think it is," said Isabella.

Emily felt like they were ganging up on her. Why couldn't Olive see that Isabella was lazy and needed to be pushed into doing good deeds?

"Isabella might be stronger than you think," said the olive tree.

"That's right!" declared Isabella triumphantly.

"And Isabella might even be stronger than she thinks," added Olive. "Her heartwood is stronger than she knows."

Emily was confused and irritated and hurt. If Olive really understood their family, she'd see that Isabella was lazy. Emily saw herself as the strong one—the true servant of the family.

And Aiden? He was always running off to play sports. Emily held bake sales to raise money, she worked on food drives, and she went on mission trips. So, why was Olive talking about Isabella having strong heartwood?

She should be talking about me! Emily thought.

"We better be quiet now," whispered Red the Fox, walking directly behind Malachi. "Malachi's staff is sensing a fungus among us."

"His staff senses a fungus?" Emily said.

"Just look." The little fox pointed at Malachi's staff.

Red was right. Several strange growths had appeared on the upper half of the staff. They looked like orange, mushroom-like things—about a dozen of them growing on the side of the wooden staff.

"Those growths mean the fungus is nearby," explained Red.

Motioning with his hand, Malachi directed them to a large, fallen tree, which had the same orange growths on it. Everyone crouched behind the log—everyone except Olive, that is. She was too tall to hide behind a log. So, she stood perfectly still and tried to blend in with the rest of the forest.

Emily peeked her head above the log and spotted something large moving silently through the trees. At first, she couldn't get a good look at it. But then this "thing" moved into a clearing and let out a roar—the same bellow she had heard in the middle of the night.

A chill ran up and down her spine.

THE HUMONGOUS FUNGUS

Isabella had never heard or seen anything so terrible. The Humongous Fungus was a shapeless blob of gooey, growing fungi, and it must've stood fifteen feet tall. It walked on three thick legs, but the creature kept changing shape. First it had two arms, then three, then four.

The giant fungus strode up to a tree and wrapped its body around the trunk. It was hugging the tree, but not a friendly kind of hug. The fungus looked more like a pro wrestler, squeezing the tree to pieces.

Suddenly, there was a terrible **CRACK!** The giant fungus released its hold and stepped back, revealing a gaping wound in the tree's side. Then the Humongous Fungus stuck a gooey hand into the crack and began stealing food from the tree.

Olive told me I could leave Redvale any time I wanted, Isabella thought. *Now would be a good time.*

However, Isabella felt bad for the wounded tree. How could she leave Redvale without at least trying to help? But what could she do to stop such a huge, horrible monster?

Suddenly, a thought slipped into her mind, as mysterious as a mushroom. She stood up.

"Isabella, what are you doing? Stay down," hissed Aiden.

Isabella looked over at Malachi, but he didn't say a word. He silently nodded his head, as if to encourage her. Then, ever so slowly, Isabella started to walk toward the injured tree.

The giant fungus turned and stared at her with evil eyes. Isabella came to a stop and wondered if she was acting crazy. But Malachi had nodded! That must mean something. That must mean he approved of what she was doing!

Looking over her shoulder, she saw the others peer at her with disbelieving eyes. Red made a move to join her, but Malachi put a hand on the fox's shoulder and whispered something to him. Then Malachi handed his staff to Red, and the fox bounded from behind the log.

Red held out the staff to Isabella. "Here. Take."

Malachi was giving his wooden staff to her? Isabella couldn't believe he was trusting it with her. She wrapped her fingers around the staff and felt power surging into her hands.

Red scampered back to the log.

Turning back to face the Humongous Fungus, Isabella began walking again, one slow step at a time. The Fungus had three eyes, which moved around on its shape-shifting body, and he peered at her with two of them. The third eye stared in a different direction.

The creature gave out a low growl, like a warning, but Isabella kept coming.

"It's okay, it's okay," she said gently. It was like the time she came across an unfriendly, growling dog and spoke to it in a calming way. The dog let her alone, and she prayed to God that the Humongous Fungus would do the same.

As Isabella stepped closer to the Fungus and the injured tree, she noticed a boulder a few feet to her right. For some reason, it made her think about the story she learned at church about Moses, who led the Israelites into the wilderness. The Israelites got angry and thirsty, demanding water. In fact, they were so angry that they were about to kill Moses, when the prophet of God used his staff to touch a rock. Instantly, water came pouring out.

The staff of Moses brought water from a rock! Isabella stared at Malachi's staff. Could it possibly be?

As she walked toward the rock, the Humongous Fungus growled even louder. He started to charge toward her, but then he stopped. It was a fake charge, an attempt to scare her. He was doing a good job at that.

Isabella reached out the staff and tapped the rock with it. Nothing happened.

As if that wasn't bad enough, the Humongous Fungus began to stomp toward her, constantly changing shape with every step. She tapped the rock again.

Nothing! Why did I think this would work?

"Please, God, please save me," Isabella said. This time, she jammed the staff into the rock like a sword, and as it sank into the stone, the ground started shaking beneath her feet.

Isabella had never felt an earthquake, but this was probably what it was like. She nearly lost her balance as the ground rose and fell like a wave. Then the rock began to shake, and a little trickle of water appeared on the stone, like a tiny teardrop.

All at once, the teardrop became a gurgling fountain. A small amount of water spouted from the rock like a drinking fountain.

The Humongous Fungus took a step backward, as if afraid.

Then, with startling suddenness, the water broke through, bursting from the rock. But this wasn't normal water. It seemed to be alive. Some of the water took the shape of little people!

One of the "water people" walked right up to Isabella. It appeared to be a water girl. After bowing, the water girl pointed at Isabella, then at herself, and then at the cracked tree.

Isabella understood.

Crouching, Isabella held out both her hands, and the water girl climbed into them. The water felt cool on her skin. With the girl balanced in her hands, Isabella walked toward the cracked tree.

Again, the Humongous Fungus stepped backward, as if afraid of the water.

When Isabella reached the wounded tree, she lifted the water girl up to the crack. Then the little girl leaped from her hands, like jumping from a diving board, and disappeared into the crack with a splash.

Isabella couldn't believe it. The crack suddenly became a bit smaller.

Feeling something wet on her shoes, she looked down and was shocked to see another water girl tugging on her pants leg. Isabella lifted her up, and she too dove into the crack.

Once again, the crack became smaller.

Isabella couldn't keep from laughing. There was an entire line of water people by this time, waiting for her to lift them up. One by one, they dove into the crack.

"Isabella, this is incredible!" came Emily's voice.

Turning, Isabella saw that the others had come out of the hiding spot behind the log. They stood around her, staring wide-eyed at the water people.

"Can we help?" asked Aiden.

"Of course. All for one and one for all!"

So, Red, Aiden, and Emily also put out their hands and lifted the water people, one by one. Even after the crack in the tree had completely healed, the water people kept coming. It was too much fun to stop now. In fact, it was so much fun that Isabella forgot all about the Humongous Fungus.

When she finally remembered the creature, she looked around and grinned. The Fungus was gone. It had completely vanished.

TO BE CONTINUED ON PAGE 127.

DAY 13

JESUS SERVED WHEN HE SAW OUR HEARTS AND HURTS

DOWN TO THE STUMP

After a tree is cut down, the part of the trunk left standing is called the stump. In the center of the stump is the tree's core, or heartwood. The wood around the core grows in layers or rings, which we call "annual rings."

Each year, a new ring of wood grows. So, if you count the number of rings, you get a pretty good idea of how old the tree was when it was cut down.

How old do you think the tree stumps are below? Try to count their annual rings.

How many annual rings?

How many annual rings?

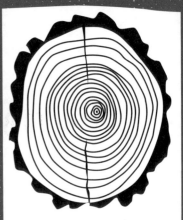

How many annual rings?

To learn more about a tree, you must peer inside it. And as the following story shows, it's the same for people. It's wrong to judge people based on what you see on the outside. You must dig deeper. You must look at what's inside a person's heart.

FIGHTING FOR FAIRNESS

One day, when Ralph Lazo went to high school, he discovered that all the Japanese students were mysteriously gone. He was told the Japanese students had been ordered to leave their jobs, homes, and schools to go live in a special area where the U.S. government could watch them. The year was 1942, and the United States was at war with Japan, Italy, and Germany.

Ralph, who was seventeen years old at the time, didn't understand why the Japanese students were told to do this. It seemed unfair, so he decided to go with them. He told his parents he was leaving for summer camp, but instead, he took a bus and headed to the camp where Japanese were being housed.

Overall, about 12,000 Japanese Americans were sent to the camps during World War II. The government worried there were Japanese spies among them, so they mistreated the Japanese Americans out of fear.

Ralph was the only person in history admitted into these camps who was not Japanese American or the spouse of one. But no one stopped him, and no guards even noticed. While Ralph lived in the camp, he served the people. He wanted them to have fair treatment. But, most of all, he wanted them to be able to return home.

After the war ended and Ralph grew up, he spoke about what happened in the camps. He fought for fairness. He wanted the government to admit that what it did was wrong. You can't lock people up because they look a certain way.

DON'T JUDGE A BOOK BY ITS COVER

Later, the American government admitted it was wrong to treat Japanese Americans unfairly during the war. Ever since, no race or people group has been rounded up and forced to live in camps in the U.S.

To truly know a person, we must look at them from the inside. You can't judge a person by looking at their skin color or weight or height or any other external feature. To put it another way: We learn people's stories through friendship.

There's an old expression: "Don't judge a book by its cover." You don't really know how good a book is until you open it up and begin reading the story. It's the same with people. You need to know their story before you truly know them.

Jesus is your friend. He knows everything about you. In fact, Matthew 10:30 (NIV) says, **"even the very hairs on your head are all numbered."** Imagine! God knows exactly how many hairs you have on your head. And you thought it was tricky counting annual rings on a tree stump!

Nobody is perfect, including Ralph Lazo. He lied to his parents and disappeared for days before they found out what happened to him. Ralph still had some growing up to do, but that didn't stop him from learning about others and serving them.

You can still serve, even when you are not at your strongest or best.

In addition, Ralph was young, but it didn't matter. Even when you are young, you can make a difference. You can serve people at any age.

You might say that people have "annual rings" just like trees. Every year, our planet circles the sun. So, Ralph had circled the sun only seventeen times when he set out to serve the Japanese Americans in those camps.

It goes to show that young people like you can still show compassion and love to others. Let's do it!

CHALLENGE—GETTING TO KNOW YOU

Your challenge is to learn something about a person—something you cannot tell from the outside. Ask them questions. Get to know their story. Then use that information to find a way to serve them!

RED ALERT!

Jesus reached out to all kinds of people, even those thought of as enemies. For example, he talked with a "Samaritan" woman. The Jews of Jesus's time thought Samaritans were unclean because they married non-Jews. But that didn't stop Jesus from talking with them!

DAY 14

JESUS SERVED WHEN HE WAS TIRED

CHORES—LIKES AND DISLIKES

Rank these chores from 1 to 10, with 1 being your least favorite chore and 10 being your favorite.

_____ Walking the dog

_____ Mopping the floor

_____ Unloading the dishwasher

_____ Picking up toys

_____ Clearing the table

_____ Dusting

_____ Washing the car

_____ Cleaning bathrooms

_____ Folding laundry

_____ Doing yardwork

A MICKEY MISTAKE

In the Disney short video, *Mickey and the Sorcerer's Hat*, Mickey Mouse got himself into big trouble. He took his master's magic hat and used its power to get his chores done without lifting a finger.

Unfortunately, the magic went wildly out of control. What started out as a simple job of mopping the floor turned into a huge flood and a tidal wave of chaos. When the master returned, all it took was a few waves of his arms to fix the trouble that Mickey caused.

The real power is not in things but in the person. The Sorcerer didn't need to put on his hat before he could fix the mess Mickey had caused. Instead, he simply raised his hands, and the water disappeared. The hat didn't make the magician powerful; the magician made the hat powerful.

Mickey Mouse is a fictional character, but the power of Jesus is real. Miracles are not mere magic tricks. They are created by God.

Like Mickey, Jesus's disciples found themselves in big trouble, with water sloshing everywhere, and they didn't know what to do. Here is what happened.

> **"Then he [Jesus] got in the boat, his disciples with him. The next thing they knew, they were in a severe storm. Waves were crashing into the boat—and he was sound asleep! They roused him, pleading, 'Master, save us! We're going down!'**

> **"Jesus reprimanded them. 'Why are you such cowards, such faint-hearts?' Then he stood up and told the wind to be silent, the sea to quiet down: 'Silence!' The sea became smooth as glass.**

"The men rubbed their eyes, astonished. 'What's going on here? Wind and sea stand up and take notice at his command!'" Matthew 8:23-27 (MSG)

Note that Jesus didn't need a magic hat or special words to perform His miracles. He is an all-powerful God who can help us without tricks or magical words.

JESUS DIDN'T TIRE OF SERVING

Did you notice another thing in this story? Jesus was asleep when the storm struck! When the disciples woke Him, Jesus didn't complain. He didn't tell them to quiet down and let Him go back to sleep. He saw their fear, and He calmed them down. He served them. He put their fears above His need for a nap.

You are human, so you will get tired, bored, or frustrated when you try to serve others. Like Mickey Mouse, you'll be tempted to find a shortcut in your work. You might even give up or not offer to help in the first place.

Thankfully, we have a Savior who never gave up on you. Jesus didn't stop serving even when it became hard or when He got tired.

Being sleepy wasn't the worst thing Jesus would face in His life. He would be beaten, nailed to a cross, and blamed for all the world's sins. When Jesus was nailed to the cross, Satan thought he had won. Even the thief crucified next to Him asked Him why He didn't save Himself.

Despite the pain and the taunting, Jesus rose again, defeated death, and lives so we can have new life in Him. Jesus served, even when it hurt.

OPERATION OTHERS

Jesus served us when it was hardest for Him. This gives us hope because we can trust Him when things are out of control. He will never give up on us, even when it seems like we're sinking in a storm.

When we fully understand that God loves us deeply, it gives us the energy to serve when we're tired, bored, or overwhelmed. In fact, helping someone might be the exact thing that helps us feel better. When we serve, we stop thinking about ourselves all the time.

When we feel like we've run all out of gas, we can rely on God's power. During hard times, we can still serve others. We don't need a sorcerer's hat. We just need Jesus.

CHALLENGE—CHORE TIME!

Serving sometimes involves doing chores for others. So, do a household chore for someone today. Choose one that you would not usually have to do. But make sure you ask a parent/guardian if it would be okay before you chip in!

Write down the chore you did below.

_____

_____

DAY 15

JESUS SERVED TO BE AN EXAMPLE

FOLLOW THE LEADER

Sing the song *Following the Leader* by Bobby Driscoll and Paul Collins. Or, if you would rather, watch a YouTube clip of the song from the Disney movie *Peter Pan*. Here are the words:

Following the leader, the leader, the leader.
We're following the leader
Wherever he may go.

Tee dum, tee dee, a teedle ee do tee day.
Tee dum, tee dee, it's part of the game we play.
Tee dum, tee dee, the words are easy to say.
Just a teedle ee dum, a teedle ee do tee day.

Tee dum, tee dee, a teedle ee do tee dum.
We're one for all, and all of us out for fun.
We march in line and follow the other one.
With a teedle ee do, a teedle ee do tee dum.

If you have time, also play the game Follow the Leader with friends. Pick one person to be the leader, while everyone else stands in single file behind him or her. Copy everything you see the person in front of you doing. Take turns being the leader.

WHAT KIND OF LEADER WAS JESUS?

In this world, many leaders expect to be followed. Some leaders will punish people who do not follow them. And in certain countries, you can be thrown in jail for just criticizing the leader.

Even Peter Pan wasn't the best of leaders. Although the Lost Boys followed him, Peter didn't always make the best choices.

So, what kind of leader was Jesus?

Jesus was in charge of *everything*. As it says in John 13:3, **"Jesus knew that the Father had put him in complete charge of everything, that he came from God and was on his way back to God." (MSG)**

So, if Jesus was in charge of everything, did He force everyone to serve Him? You would think so. But if you read John 13, you'll see that Jesus did something completely different.

> **"So he got up from the supper table, set aside his robe, and put on an apron. Then he poured water into a basin and began to wash the feet of the disciples, drying them with his apron. When he got to Simon Peter, Peter said, 'Master, *you* wash *my* feet?'" John 13:4-6 (MSG)**

Hold on! Jesus washed His disciples' feet? Even Peter thought this was strange. He asked, with a puzzled look, **"Master, *you* wash *my* feet?"**

The word disciple means "follower." So, shouldn't the disciples—the followers—be washing the feet of their leader?

Washing feet was a dirty job. After hiking across dusty roads in sandals all day, feet can get dirty and smelly. That's why, during Bible days, one of the first things you did after coming indoors was have your feet washed, usually by a servant. Washing feet was as bad as taking out the trash. No one wanted to do it.

DIRTY JOBS

Jesus showed His disciples that being a leader meant doing dirty jobs. And one of those jobs was washing feet. The disciples thought this was strange. They were confused.

> **"Jesus answered, 'You don't understand now what I'm doing, but it will be clear enough to you later.'**
>
> **"Peter persisted, 'You're not going to wash my feet—ever!'**
>
> **"Jesus said, 'If I don't wash you, you can't be part of what I'm doing.'"**
> **John 13:7-8 (MSG)**

But Jesus didn't just wash His followers' feet. He also washed them completely clean of sin—and He'll do the same for us. In fact, we cannot follow Jesus unless He first washes us clean from sin.

God's Kingdom is different than our kingdom. In God's Kingdom, the King takes out the trash! And unless Jesus takes out our trash—unless we let Him get rid of all our disgusting, smelly sins—we cannot be a part of His Kingdom.

We must also learn to serve each other. As Jesus went on to say...

> **"'So if I, the Master and Teacher, washed your feet, you must now wash each other's feet. I've laid down a pattern for you. What I've done, you do.'" John 13:14-15 (MSG)**

After Jesus removes your sin, He invites you to be His disciple. This time, sing the song *Following the Leader*, but replace the word "following" with "discipling."

> *"Jesus disciples His people, His people, His people.*
> *Jesus disciples His people wherever they may go."*

One line in the song also says, "It's part of the game we play." But following Jesus is not a game. Games have an end and then you put all the pieces back in the box. But following Jesus lasts a lifetime. It's an adventure! So, let's go!

CHALLENGE—WISE UP AND CLEAN UP!

Wash something for someone today. Clean up after someone else's spills or wipe up under your baby sister's highchair. You can also clean the family car, dinner dishes, the family pet, or a friend's bike.

As you wash, sing this song:

> *Following the Savior, the Savior, the Savior*
> *We're following the Savior*
> *Wherever He may go!*

DAY 16

JESUS SERVED EVEN WHEN HE WASN'T THANKED

SICK DAYS

When you feel sick, what makes you feel better? Mark all the things you do when you are sick.

- [ ] Take my temperature
- [ ] Snuggle under a fuzzy blanket
- [ ] Take a bath
- [ ] Take medicine
- [ ] Use an ice pack
- [ ] Eat chicken noodle soup
- [ ] Drink Sprite
- [ ] Use a heating pad
- [ ] Get a back rub
- [ ] Take a nap
- [ ] Drink orange juice
- [ ] Watch a show

It's nice to be cared for when you are sick. But imagine what it would feel like if you caught an illness and had to move away from everyone you loved. During the pandemic, this is what happened to many people who had to stay away from others. In ancient Israel, this is also what happened to people who had a disease called leprosy. They had to be separated from other people. People can still get leprosy today, but it is not as dangerous as it used to be. We now have medicine to cure it.

The Bible tells us a story of ten men with leprosy. Because they had to stay away from people, they could only shout to Jesus from far off. They begged Him to heal them. He was their only hope. Interestingly, this is the only healing in the Bible where most of the story comes *after* the miracle. Read about what happened.

> **"It happened that as he [Jesus] made his way toward Jerusalem, he crossed over the border between Samaria and Galilee. As he entered a village, ten men, all lepers, met him. They kept their distance but raised their voices, calling out, 'Jesus, Master, have mercy on us!'**
>
> **"Taking a good look at them, he said, 'Go, show yourselves to the priests.'**
>
> **"They went and while still on their way, became clean. One of them, when he realized that he was healed, turned around and came back, shouting his gratitude, glorifying God. He kneeled at Jesus' feet, so grateful. He couldn't thank him enough—and he was a Samaritan.**
>
> **"Jesus said, 'Were not ten healed? Where are the nine? Can none be found to come back and give glory to God except this outsider?' Then he said to him, 'Get up. On your way. Your faith has healed and saved you.'" Luke 17:11-19 (MSG)**

A THANKLESS JOB

The ten lepers were healed, but only one returned to Jesus to say thank you. That's sad, but not unusual.

Sometimes, when you do things for others, they will not even notice. When others don't care about your work or what you are doing, it can hurt. You might even want to give up on ever doing helpful things. But Jesus didn't demand to be thanked before healing the ten lepers.

Jesus wants us to have thankful hearts. He wants us to be grateful for the good in our lives. But He doesn't stop serving and helping us just because we're not thankful. No one thanked Jesus when He died on the cross. It was a thankless and lonely death.

Thankfully, we never have to worry about whether people thank us or not. God sees what we do, just as Jesus saw how the one leper came to Him with thankfulness in His heart. Getting praise from God keeps our focus on what really matters. We won't be bothered when people are not thankful or don't notice the things we do.

It's not about us! God sees what you do, and you are pleasing to Him!

> **"God doesn't miss anything. He knows perfectly well all the love you've shown him by helping needy Christians, and that you keep at it." Hebrews 6:10 (MSG)**

CHALLENGE—THE BOO-BOO BAG

A boo-boo is what people call a minor injury, cut, or scrape that needs healing. When a boo-boo happens, you need something to help take care of it.

Make a bag and fill it with first-aid supplies for a family, classroom, team, or any other group of people. For example, you can give one to a family shelter, people who do home care, office workers, or those on mission trips.

Be a first-aid kid with a first-aid kit. Collect some or all of the following:

First-Aid Kit
- Quart-sized Ziploc bags
- First aid cream
- Band-Aids
- Gauze
- Washcloth
- Elastic bandage
- Cotton swabs
- Antiseptic towelettes
- Small scissors
- Permanent marker
- Caladryl lotion
- Q-tips

Decide who you are going to make a Boo-boo Bag for. This will help you avoid buying too many supplies. Then, go together as a family to buy the supplies at a dollar store or pharmacy. You can also order supplies from Amazon and assemble them together as a family.

RED ALERT!

The Hebrew word "beth" means "house." That's why so many town names in the Bible include "beth"— Bethany (house of figs), Bethsaida (house of fish), Bethlehem (house of bread), Beth-Shean (house of quiet and rest), and on and on.

DAY 17

JESUS SERVED WHEN PEOPLE WERE SUFFERING

BARKING UP THE WRONG TREE

Before we had photographs, people had to draw nature by hand. So, grab your crayon box and look up each tree's bark pattern. Then try to copy these patterns in the boxes. Pay attention to the color, pattern, and lines.

CHERRY	HONEY LOCUST	FLOWERING DOGWOOD

EASTERN REDCEDAR	FRANKLINIA	WEEPING WILLOW

Bark is the tough outside layer that covers the tree like skin. It protects the tree from insect damage, disease, and harsh weather. Some bark is as thin as a sheet of paper, while other bark grows to be several feet thick.

Young trees, like a kid's skin, have smooth bark. But as trees age, their trunk becomes more wrinkled and even cracks. A tree's trunk also supports its branches like your skeleton holds up your body. Thick bark means protection and safety for the tree.

THICK SKIN, THIN SKIN

Have you ever heard the phrase "thick skin"? This expression doesn't have anything to do with the skin on our bodies. It's talking about our feelings.

If someone has "thick skin," it means they don't get upset by the words or actions of others very quickly. The opposite, "thin skin," describes someone who is sensitive to the words and actions of others. For example, someone might say you have thin skin if you hate to be teased or if it hurts your feelings when people boo your favorite team.

When you are hurt, it's tempting to create a hard shell around your feelings, like thick skin. You try to hide your feelings, rarely sharing how you really feel. This "shell" protects you from people's mean words or actions, but it also creates a wall around your heart.

Thick skin can keep you from feeling anything. Sometimes we even make our skins so thick that love cannot flow out from us. This kind of thick skin keeps us from loving or caring for people. It keeps everyone out, even people we love.

In the following story, people got angry at Jesus for serving. Read the story and then answer this question: Did Jesus have thick skin?

> "Back in the boat, Jesus and the disciples recrossed the sea to Jesus' hometown. They were hardly out of the boat when some men carried a paraplegic on a stretcher and set him down in front of them. Jesus, impressed by their bold belief, said to the paraplegic, 'Cheer up, son. I forgive your sins.' Some religion scholars whispered, 'Why, that's blasphemy!'

"Jesus knew what they were thinking, and said, 'Why this gossipy whispering? Which do you think is simpler: to say, 'I forgive your sins,' or, 'Get up and walk'? Well, just so it's clear that I'm the Son of Man and authorized to do either, or both. . . .' At this he turned to the paraplegic and said, 'Get up. Take your bed and go home.' And the man did it. The crowd was awestruck, amazed and pleased that God had authorized Jesus to work among them this way." Matthew 9:1-8 (MSG)

So, did Jesus have thick skin in this story? It depends on how you look at it. He didn't seem bothered when the religious scholars gossiped against Him, but He also did not shut people out. He kept showing love.

You might say, therefore, that His skin wasn't too thick or too thin. He didn't let the criticisms of others prevent Him from doing what was right. But He also didn't put a shell around His heart to keep Him from loving.

Jesus hates it when our feelings are hurt, but He does not want us to have thick skin around our hearts. Jesus has a soft heart for everyone, and that includes you. 1 Peter says, **"Most important of all, continue to show deep love for each other, for love covers a multitude of sins." 1 Peter 4:8 (NLT)**

In other words, God wants us to have a soft heart—and a strong heart. Strong hearts don't get as hurt by mean words or rude actions, while soft hearts see the hurt and pain in others.

As we discussed on Day 13, the tree's 'heartwood' is found in the center of the trunk. It is a cluster of fibers connected by a glue-like substance called "lignin." The heartwood can be as strong as steel. As the U.S. Forest Service says, a piece 12 inches long can hold a weight of 20 tons!

Jesus's heart was that strong. He could take on the weight of the world—and not be crushed by it. He could still feel for others when they suffered. He could still heal their wounds.

CHALLENGE—BARK RUBBINGS

When we talk about trees, we often study their size, fruit, flowers, or shape of the leaves. But we often forget about the bark. The cool thing about tree bark is you can examine it any time of the year.

Try making "bark prints" by placing paper against the bark and rubbing it with crayons. The texture will come through. Use those bark rubbings to make cards or bookmarks for others. Finally, add the Bible verse written below. Give that bookmark to someone who could use an encouraging word.

"Most important of all, continue to show deep love for each other, for love covers a multitude of sins." 1 Peter 4:8 (NLT)

RED ALERT!

When Aaron threw down his staff in front of Pharaoh, the wooden staff turned into a snake. In response, Pharaoh's magicians also threw down their staffs, which turned into snakes. But the snake of Aaron's staff devoured the magicians' snakes, showing God's power over evil. (Exodus 7:8-13)

DAY 18

JESUS SERVED WHEN TIMES WERE TOUGH

I'M STUMPED!

When we think about serving, we usually imagine the strong helping the weak, the healthy helping the sick, the big helping the small, or the happy helping the sad. But if that were true, that means we would be able to help only when we feel stronger, healthier, bigger, or happier than others.

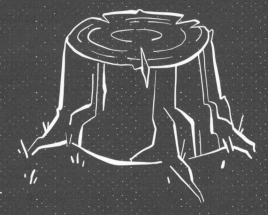

Perhaps we're like tree stumps, which can help even when they're weak. At first glance, a tree stump seems useless. When you see a stump, you usually think of a dead tree. After all, a stump cannot make food because it doesn't have leaves. The chlorophyll in leaves turns the water and nutrients into food for the rest of the tree.

It is hard to imagine a stump being any use at all in a forest.

Many stumps do die. But scientists have found that some of them are still alive. This is because other trees around the stump keep it alive through their roots beneath the ground. As a result, old stumps can live hundreds of years without leaves.

Scientists also think the trees helping the stumps might be children of that stump. In other words, stumps are like parents and grandparents, who are still part of the tree community. Even though stumps cannot make their own food or share anymore, they can store memories about the weather in their roots. The other trees use this knowledge to predict when winter or spring are coming.

The tree stump shows that even when a tree is the weakest, it can be strong. The same is true for you—and the same was true for Jesus. He was strong, even at His weakest moment.

ALL ALONE

One of the saddest moments for Jesus was when He prayed in the Garden of Gethsemane just hours before He would be arrested and nailed to the cross. When He was arrested, Jesus seemed weak, small, and sad.

Seeing Jesus like this made Peter really angry. He pulled out his sword and sliced off the ear of one of the men arresting Jesus. Read about what Jesus did next:

> **"When Jesus' followers saw what was going to happen, they said, 'Lord, should we strike with our swords?' And one of them struck the servant of the high priest, cutting off his right ear.**
>
> **"But Jesus answered, 'No more of this!' And he touched the man's ear and healed him." Luke 22:49-51 (NIV)**

Even while Jesus was being arrested, He still served other people. He healed the servant of the priest arresting Him. The people arresting Jesus hated Him, yet Jesus still cared about them.

Jesus showed that it's possible to serve, even when you feel your weakest.

Have you ever felt smaller or weaker than others?

Maybe you don't get as many gifts at Christmas as your friends, or you are shy and quiet. But even when we have less than others or are shyer than our friends, we can still serve. When people are rude or unkind to us, remember how Jesus treated those arresting Him.

Jesus loves you just as much as the man whose ear was cut off—and He comes to you when you feel small, unimportant, sad, and weak. By becoming a man and dying on the cross, Jesus made Himself smaller and weaker, and He experienced more pain than you ever will feel. Yet, His love is big enough to take all our sins away and give us new life.

When we feel "cut down," like a tree that is only a stump, remember this truth. There's still life in that stump. Jesus still loves us and still heals us and serves us. In His eyes, we're as precious as the largest redwood.

We have a glorious God who reigns on high! Isn't that tree-mendous?

CHALLENGE—THE EXCUSE MONSTER

Here are some popular excuses that kids use to get out of chores:

- "My dog ate my homework!"
- "This grocery bag is too heavy!"
- "I don't feel like going to school."
- "Someone else will clean up my mess."

- "I don't have time to clean my room!"
- "I'm not helping. It's not my turn."
- "The tub overflowed because I just forgot."
- "I already did my job. I don't have to do yours too."

Don't become an Excuse Monster! Fill out the sentence below:

EVEN WHEN I AM FEELING _____

I CAN STILL SERVE BY _____.

RED ALERT!

God does not give up on us. When things are tough, He can turn our lives around, like planting trees in a desert. As Isaiah 41:17-20 says, God will even make acacia, myrtle, olive, juniper, fir, and cypress trees grow in the desert. And if He can bring hope to a barren desert, He can bring hope to you.

DAY 19

JESUS SERVED WHEN IT WASN'T FAIR

DIRTY, DANGEROUS JOBS

In the Asian country of Pakistan, at least 80 percent of the street sweepers, janitors, and sewer workers are Christians, according to a 2020 article from Persecution International. In fact, the Pakistani army once placed a newspaper ad that said: "Sewer Cleaners Wanted in Pakistan: Only Christians Need Apply."

Why do they want only Christians? It's because those are dangerous, dirty jobs. Almost all sewer cleaners have skin and breathing problems because of contacting dangerous materials. Many sewer workers in Pakistan die.

Pakistan has what is called a "caste system," which ranks people according to their importance. The people who converted to Christianity were already at the bottom of the caste system. They lived in poor neighborhoods and took the worst jobs—like cleaning sewers.

In Pakistan, you won't find anyone who wants to be a sewer worker when they grow up. But if your father or mother has one of these jobs, you would be forced to follow in their footsteps. It doesn't matter if you're smart or work hard. You're stuck.

This is terribly unfair.

When the poor in Pakistan heard that Jesus loves all people, no matter if they were rich or poor, they couldn't believe their ears. The good news of Jesus gave hope to the poorest of the poor. Despite the horrible jobs and terrible living conditions, Christianity is growing among the poor in Pakistan.

Although it isn't fair that these people receive less than others, they are joyful in their Lord Jesus, and they serve others gladly. It is hard enough to serve when your life is okay. Imagine serving when things are unfair!

THE UNFAIRNESS OF THE CROSS

When Jesus was on the cross, He had the power to save Himself. People shouted at Him to prove Himself by coming down from the cross. Even the Roman soldiers challenged Him to do that, but they didn't really think He could. They were poking fun at Him.

It must have been difficult for Jesus to stay up on the cross, for He had done nothing wrong. Jesus took the sins of the whole world on Himself. He took our punishment in our place. This is something only God could do. No human could have survived that.

But the soldiers weren't the only ones who told Jesus to save Himself. Read about another person who challenged Him in the verses below.

"The soldiers also came up and mocked him. They offered him wine vinegar and said, 'If you are the king of the Jews, save yourself.'

"There was a written notice above him, which read: THIS IS THE KING OF THE JEWS.

"One of the criminals who hung there hurled insults at him: 'Aren't you the Messiah? Save yourself and us!'

"But the other criminal rebuked him. 'Don't you fear God,' he said, 'since you are under the same sentence? We are punished justly, for we are getting what our deeds deserve. But this man has done nothing wrong.'

"Then he said, 'Jesus, remember me when you come into your kingdom.'

"Jesus answered him, 'Truly I tell you, today you will be with me in paradise.'" **Luke 23:36-43 (NIV)**

One of the prisoners on the cross teased Jesus, but the other one saw the unfairness of what was happening. Jesus "has done nothing wrong," he said.

Serving is not always going to be fair. When we serve, we give our energy, time, and talents to others. Even though we are not supposed to get anything back, it is still tempting to get upset when we don't get payback or praise. It doesn't seem fair—that is, until we think about Jesus.

Jesus faced the most unfair thing of all. He was the only perfect person to ever live. Yet He took on everyone's sin on the cross. Jesus was separated from God and paid the price for us. If things were fair, we would face death and be in hell forever. What an awful ending. Thank goodness God is not worried about fairness!

Jesus faced unfair situations so we could be loved and saved!

"All suffering, all pain, all emptiness, all disappointment is a seed: sow it in God and He will, finally, bring a crop of joy from it."

— Eugene Peterson

CHALLENGE—THE FAIRNESS FACTOR

Do something today that feels unfair.

- Give a friend a push on the swing without asking for your turn.
- Do your sibling's chore without expecting any payback.
- Help your mom without her having to ask you.

When you serve, don't worry about fairness. God promises to make everything right!

RED ALERT!

When Romans killed people on a cross, it is called "crucifixion." Romans used the cross to kill people until Constantine banned it in the Fourth Century AD. Constantine was the first Christian emperor in Rome.

HOW DID SERVE?

JESUS

THE FOREST OF REDVALE

PART 4

Aiden couldn't believe his eyes.

A small water person leaped from the palms of his hands and splashed against the tree. Then Aiden turned and scooped up another handful of water, which took the shape of a boy!

"This water is alive!" he shouted gleefully.

Aiden also couldn't believe his eyes when he examined the injured tree. Where the water splashed against the tree, the crack had completely disappeared.

This is more fun than a water park, Aiden thought, as he and the others carried the Living Water to the injured tree for another fifteen minutes. Then the water gushing from the rock suddenly stopped flowing, as if someone turned off a faucet.

Aiden ran his hand across the tree, where the large crack once split the wood.

"How did this water heal the tree?" he asked.

"It wasn't the water that did it," Malachi said. "When you serve, you heal, and all of you were servants, thanks to Isabella's example."

"And thanks to your staff," Emily said to Malachi. "Why didn't you tell us your staff was so much more than a walking stick?"

"My staff is made from wood in the Forest of Redvale," Malachi said. "It's connected to these trees, so it has abilities here that it doesn't in other places. But, once again, the staff didn't do the healing. It was Isabella's servant heart."

"Your heartwood has become even stronger because of what you did," added Olive, brushing a branch across Isabella's hair. "You showed great compassion in the face of great danger."

"Even more importantly, you didn't just *feel* compassion," said Malachi. "You put your compassion into action."

"You were very brave in facing the Humongous Fungus," said Jesse, shocking everyone. It was a big deal when Jesse gave someone a compliment.

Red the Fox bounced on top of Jesse's head and threw out his arms. "You showed humongous love, Isabella!"

Malachi ran a hand across the healed tree. "The Fungus is fearless, except when it sees a Giver, like Isabella."

"We won't be seeing him for a long time," said Red.

"Everybody has cracks of some sort that need healing," said Olive. "Even humans like you have cracks, although you can't see them. But Living Water heals all wounds."

Malachi thumped his staff on the ground to get everyone's attention. "As much fun as the Living Water has been, if we want to plant those acorns before dark, we better get moving,"

So, the band of brothers and sisters took one last look at the healed tree, taking turns running their hands across the bark. Then the march began, following a narrow trail through the Forest of Redvale.

"That was really cool what you did back there," Aiden said, slipping beside Isabella. "Were you afraid?"

"Terrified," said his older sister. "But I don't know...I think God was urging me on. I kept picturing how Jesus washed the feet of the disciples on the night before He died. If the God of the Universe can get down on His hands and knees and wash the smelly toes of His disciples, I figured I could serve that poor tree."

"Well...I won't ever tease you about being lazy again." Aiden gave Isabella a gentle punch on the shoulder. "And I also won't ask you to wash my smelly feet."

Isabella grinned. "Good. Facing the Humongous Fungus was bad. But facing your toes? That would be a hundred times worse."

After a pause, Isabella told Aiden, "You know, Emily wasn't wrong when she said I was lazy. But there's something about coming to Redvale. It changes me."

"It changes all of us," said Aiden.

Aiden and Isabella exchanged smiles and pressed ahead. The path split off in different branches, but Aiden trusted that Malachi knew the WAY.

ED THE BEETLE

Emily thought the water people were very cool, and she was impressed by the bravery shown by Isabella. But if she were completely honest, she was also a bit jealous of her older sister.

After all, Emily wondered, wasn't she the true servant? She's been the one trying to get Isabella off the couch to serve at the church food drive. She's been the one trying to get Aiden to slow down with all his activities, so he too could help out.

But now, Isabella was getting all the praise. It didn't seem fair.

Emily was in a grouchy mood as they marched deeper into the forest. Forests can be pretty dark, especially when the trees are thick. But the Forest of Redvale became unnaturally dark, the deeper they hiked into the woods. The gloom matched her mood.

All of a sudden…music! Emily heard singing in the middle of the forest!

"Where's the music coming from?" Isabella asked before Emily had a chance to say something. Even that made Emily angry. She wanted to be the first to ask the question.

"Look over there," said Olive, pointing with one of her longest branches.

Emily squinted her eyes, trying to see what Olive was pointing at. She wanted to spot it before her sister did.

"I see it!" shouted Isabella, laughing.

"Where, where, where?" Emily asked, getting angrier by the second.

Isabella pointed. "Over by that fallen tree."

Emily still couldn't see it.

"I see it!" Aiden exclaimed. "That's the funniest thing I ever saw!"

"Where, where, where?" Frustrated, Emily stomped her foot.

Aiden laughed. "Four squirrels are singing harmony! Can't you see them?"

Finally, Emily made out the small animals in the shadows of the forest. Four squirrels stood side by side on a branch, singing an old-fashioned song together. She thought that kind of singing group was called a barbershop quartet. She was going to point that out, but Aiden beat her to it.

"I think those are called barbershop quartets," he said.

"Good job! You're exactly right," said Red.

"I knew that," mumbled Emily. Today, she just couldn't catch a break.

"As you may have noticed, this is the most musical part of the forest," said Olive. "This is where animals and birds come to make it big in the music industry."

"Animals and birds have a music industry?" Emily said, sounding grumpier than she wanted.

Olive didn't seem to mind her tone. "They do in this forest. Keep your ears open, and you'll hear all kinds of music."

She was right. As they moved deeper into the woods, Emily heard music coming from the treetops. This time, she was determined to be the first one to spot them.

"Look!" Isabella shouted. "Those birds are singing Gospel songs!"

"Don't you think I can see with my own eyes?" Emily grumbled. "With those colors, they're hard to miss."

Sure enough, two bluebirds, an oriole, and a cardinal were singing on a nearby tree branch.

"And all the trees of the field will clap their hands
The trees of the field will clap their hands,
The trees of the field will clap their hands,
While you go out with joy!"

Next, they spotted some field mice playing country music, a wild boar singing opera, and three badgers playing rock and roll. One of the badgers played a guitar, the second one played bass, and the third was on drums.

They were surrounded by every style of music. The forest rang with song.

But amid all the music, Emily suddenly heard a different sound. A sad sound. Somebody was crying. First, they met weeping willows. Then a weeping rock. Now what?

But this was her chance to show compassion. This was her chance to show she was just as brave and just as much of a servant as her sister.

Emily left the path.

She knew she should stay with the group. But she didn't want Isabella or Aiden beating her again. She could definitely hear somebody crying, and she wanted to be the one to comfort that person.

It turned out to be an insect. And not just any insect. This critter was a HUGE bug—about five feet tall. It looked to be a black beetle, and it sat on a log, crying. The beetle had handkerchiefs in each of its six hands, and he continuously removed his sunglasses to wipe his eyes and blow his nose. Do beetles have noses? This one evidently did.

"What's wrong, mister?" Emily asked, approaching carefully.

The beetle swung around to face her. "*Everything* is wrong! My friends all left me! I'm lonely!"

This was perfect! It was Emily's chance to show love to a lonely bug.

"I was in a singing group with four other beetles," the bug moaned.

Emily smiled. "What were their names—John, Paul, George, and Ringo?"

The beetle dropped one of his handkerchiefs. "How did you know?"

Emily was stunned. She had been joking, but she didn't want to say that. "What happened?"

"They kicked me out of their singing group. So, I started a Lonely Hearts Club Band, but I can't get anyone else to join. *I'm so lonely!*"

The big beetle began to blubber once again.

"There, there," said Emily, patting the beetle's back. His shell was quite hard. "I can be your friend!"

The beetle whipped his head in her direction and smiled. (She also didn't realize that beetles could smile.) "Would you really do that for me?"

"Absolutely. I know what it's like to be lonely sometimes. So, let's be friends!"

"Oh, you make me so happy!" The beetle gave her a big hug, which was kind of creepy since he had six arms. But she wasn't about to tell him that.

Emily looked around. Now would be a good time for the others to show up. They would see that she too could be compassionate. But her brother and sister were nowhere to be seen.

"By the way, I'm Emily."

"And I'm Ed."

"Pleased to meet you."

"Say, Emily, now that we're best friends, can you do me a favor?"

There was something strange in the way he spoke. But Emily didn't want to get him upset. "Sure, I'd be glad to help out."

The beetle pointed three of its hands toward the treetops. "Some bullies tossed my drum up in the branches. But I can't climb trees, so I'm very sad."

"That's okay! I'm a great climber. I'll get it for you!"

Emily could see the drum partway up a large tree. The tree had a lot of low, strong branches—perfect for climbing. So, she grabbed hold of a low branch and swung herself up. This was going to be easy.

In no time, Emily found herself on a high branch, where the drum was caught in a tangle of branches. She took hold of the drum and yanked, but it almost seemed as if the tree wouldn't let go. Was the tree the bully? Did this tree steal the poor beetle's drum?

It's possible. Not all trees were as nice as Olive.

Finally, Emily pried the drum loose from the branches. But how could she climb down while carrying a drum?

"Toss it to me!" shouted Ed the Beetle.

"But it might break!"

"Don't worry! I'll catch it!"

"Are you sure?"

"Absolutely! I've got six arms. How could I *not* catch it?"

That was an excellent point, so Emily dropped the drum down to his waiting arms. But as it plummeted to earth, the beetle stepped aside and let it crash to the ground. He didn't even try to catch it, and the drum busted open on impact.

Thousands of tiny beetles poured out from the broken drum. They looked just like Ed, except they were the size Emily was used to seeing. The beetles swarmed the nearest tree and began to drill through the bark.

That's right. Each of the tiny beetles was equipped with a power drill. And every single one of them was attacking a tree.

BEETLE-MANIA

"Where in the world did Emily go?" Isabella asked.

"She was with me a second ago," Aiden said. "Then, when I turned around, she was gone."

"She should know better than to leave the path," Malachi said with a flash of anger.

"Hold on a second," Olive said. "I'm sensing messages coming to me from nearby trees."

Isabella scratched her head. "What do you mean you're sensing messages?"

"Trees talk to each other through their roots," Olive said. "It's like an Internet beneath the soil."

"What are you hearing?" Red asked.

"It's not good. An army of bark beetles have been released not far from here. I hate to be the bearer of bad news, but the trees say that a little girl with pigtails helped to release the bark beetles."

Isabella's stomach dropped. Was there another girl in pigtails roaming the forest? It couldn't possibly be her sister!

"Emily would never do such a thing," she said.

"Follow me! I think I can lead you to the bark beetles," said Olive, heading off the path. Olive darted to the left, squeezing between trees and moving with shocking speed. It was difficult to keep up with her.

It wasn't long before Isabella heard a girl's voice shouting. Definitely Emily. Again, her stomach dropped at the thought of her little sister doing anything to harm the trees.

Bursting into the clearing, the scene before them was horrifying. An enormous beetle, the size of a human, had Emily in the clutches of his six arms. She was kicking and screaming. It certainly didn't look like Emily was helping the villain, so why did the trees accuse her of that?

Equally frightening, a swarm of tiny beetles were boring into the bark of several trees. She could hear the whir of their tiny drills.

"The big beetle is controlling the swarm of smaller bugs," said Olive. "Stop the Big Boss, and you will stop the destruction."

Isabella looked to Malachi for help. But before he could do anything, Aiden snatched the staff from Malachi's hand and sprinted toward the giant beetle.

THE STAFF OF MALACHI

Aiden figured the staff must have the power to stop the giant beetle. If it could make water gush from a rock, it could certainly stop a big insect.

Pointing the staff at the beetle, he waited for the insect to run away in fear. But the beetle, who continued to hold on to Emily, just laughed. Then he charged at Aiden and used one of his six arms to hit Aiden in the chest, slamming him backward five feet and knocking the breath out of him.

Aiden hit the ground harder than any time he had been tackled in football. This beetle would make a good linebacker.

Malachi helped Aiden rise from the ground. "You're not going to stop the beetle that way, Aiden."

"Why not? Your staff turned into a giant worm to lure away the birds. And it brought water from a rock."

"My staff is for serving, not for fighting."

Aiden looked at the piece of wood in his hands. "Then what should I do?"

Malachi stared at him, probing his eyes. As he did, it began to rain and thunder.

"Pray," Malachi whispered.

Closing his eyes, Aiden asked God to show him what to do, to show him how to serve. As lightning flashed, an image also flashed in his mind—the hazy image of a man holding a staff high above his head.

Could it be?

Leaping to his feet, Aiden held the staff in both hands and raised it above his head. *Whoa, this thing is heavier than it looks*, Aiden thought. But it worked. When he held the staff above his head, the big beetle whirled around and began growling and snarling, as if he didn't like it. He also loosened his hold on Emily, who broke from his clutches.

The drilling came to a sudden stop. All the bark beetles lowered their drills and turned to look at Aiden.

Already, Aiden's arms began to ache. Holding a staff above your head sounds simple, but it hurts! His muscles burned.

But by holding the staff high, it seemed to have a power over the beetles. The bugs packed up their drills, while the large insect kept backing away in fear.

The lightning lit up the forest with brilliant bursts of electricity. But Aiden couldn't hold up his arms any longer. It almost felt as if his muscles were tearing. So, he lowered the staff.

Bad choice. The large beetle seemed emboldened once again, and the little beetles took out their drills and returned to work.

Aiden raised the staff above his head once again.

The beetles backed off.

"I don't know how long I can do this!" Aiden shouted, as the rain came down harder.

"We'll help!" Isabella yelled, rushing to his side. She stood on tiptoes to hold up one end of the staff. Emily tried to hold up the other end, but she was too short to reach it.

"Don't worry, Emily!" said Jesse hopping up beside her. "Stand on my head!"

That worked. Emily was now tall enough to help hold up the opposite side. Relief washed across Aiden's sore muscles.

Again, the big beetle snarled and backed away, as if in fear. Again, the army of little beetles started putting away their drills in tiny tool chests. They marched off in single file, grumbling and muttering.

With Isabella and Emily's help, Aiden could feel his shoulders getting stronger and stronger. They made quite a sight, the three of them holding up the staff. All for one and one for all!

The lightning continued to flash, and the rain fell in sheets. But the water felt good on his sore muscles. It was cleansing, strengthening, and soothing all at the same time.

The lightning flashed again, blinding Aiden for just a moment. When he opened his eyes, the beetles were gone.

TO BE CONTINUED ON PAGE 171.

DAY 20

JESUS SERVED WHERE HE WAS BORN—IN BETHLEHEM

READY FOR TAKEOFF!

Get your passport ready! Fill out the spaces below with your name, birthday, place of birth, gender, and home country.

This week, we are going to be traveling with Jesus to some of the places where He served. Jesus did not travel around the world. In fact, after His family returned from Egypt when He was young, He never left Israel, a small country where He was born. His main way of getting around was by walking, so He didn't cover much ground. But that didn't stop Him from changing the world forever.

To help you picture the size of Israel, find New Jersey on a United States map. Israel is just a bit larger than New Jersey. Although we do not know every place Jesus visited, the Bible tells us about many of them, and you will be able to explore seven of those places.

Our first stop is Bethlehem, where Jesus was born. Use a tablet or map of Israel to find Bethlehem and mark it next to the correct dot on the map shown here. How far is Bethlehem from where you live?

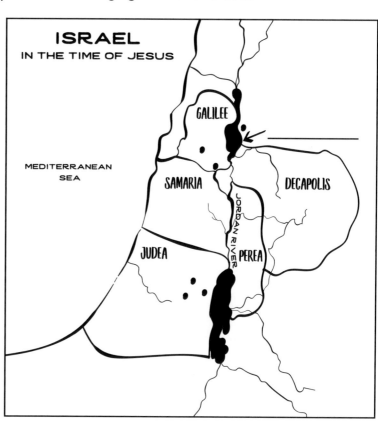

Bethlehem is _____ miles from my home.

PUTTING THE MISSION IN MISSIONARIES

Although Jesus did not travel far from His home, some people go long distances to be missionaries. These are people who carry the Gospel to faraway places. In the silly song *Please Don't Send Me to Africa*, Scott Wesley Brown sings about not wanting to be sent to Africa as a missionary. Read some of the song lyrics below or check it out on YouTube.

> *Please don't send me to Africa.*
> *I don't think I've got what it takes.*
> *I'm just a man. I'm not a Tarzan.*
> *Don't like lions, gorillas, or snakes.*
> *I'll serve you here in suburbia*
> *In my comfortable middle-class life.*
> *But please don't send me out into the bush*
> *Where the natives are restless at night.*

Missionaries do incredible work. Some provide healthcare and food, while others start churches and preach about Jesus. It is important to pray and support missionaries because they are doing hard and meaningful work. However, being a missionary is not a job for everyone. You don't have to move away from home to serve.

Most of you live right where you were born, near your parents. When you're young, you do not get to choose your home or your neighbors. Your parents pick the groups you belong to, like your church, school, or activities. But you can serve where you are, even if it seems ordinary.

WHEN ORDINARY IS EXTRAORDINARY

Bethlehem was a small, ordinary town, six miles from Jerusalem. Even though Bethlehem was not famous (yet), God chose to come as a baby to that very spot.

Three hundred years earlier, the prophet Micah wrote about Bethlehem and said that a Savior would come from that town. People did not understand what his words meant, and many of them forgot about God's promise. But some remembered. When King Herod asked His wisest men where this king would be born, they knew what Micah had written about Bethlehem. Read what they said:

> **"After Jesus was born in Bethlehem in Judea, during the time of King Herod, Magi from the east came to Jerusalem and asked, 'Where is the one who has been born king of the Jews? We saw his star when it rose and have come to worship him.'**

> **"When King Herod heard this, he was disturbed and all of Jerusalem with him. When he had called together all the people's chief priests and teachers of the law, he asked them where the Messiah was to be born. 'In Bethlehem in Judea' they replied, 'for this is what the prophet has written:**

> **"'But you, Bethlehem, in the land of Judah,**
> **are by no means least among the rulers of Judah;**
> **for out of you will come a ruler**
> **who will shepherd my people Israel.'"**
> **Matthew 2:1-6 (NIV)**

Jesus served by becoming a baby in an unimportant city. You don't have to be famous, and you don't have to be born in a big, important place to do big, important things. After all, Jesus would grow up to save the world. You can't get more important than that.

So, God needs you right where you are. You can be a missionary in your home, school, club, church, and neighborhood. Although you may not have to battle lions, gorillas, or snakes, it will not always be easy. Ask God to show you the best way to serve right where you live.

CHALLENGE—GOOD NEIGHBORS

Draw a map of your neighborhood in the space below. Draw the houses of your neighbors, and then use that map to serve someone. For example, bring cookies to a neighbor, help your mom in the garden, or make a card for your mail delivery person.

MY NEIGHBORHOOD

RED ALERT!

Joseph and Mary traveled up to 90 miles from Nazareth to Bethlehem, depending on the route they took. However, the Book of Luke never says Mary rode on a donkey, even though she's often pictured on one. A donkey could cost anywhere from two months' to two years' wages, so it was difficult for poor families to buy one. Does that mean they walked all that way? Who knows?

#SERVINGCHALLENGEKIDS

DAY 21

JESUS CARED ABOUT THE LITTLE THINGS IN CANA

A MIRACLE IN CANA

Shalom! That is how Jewish people said "hello" in Jesus's time. But before we talk more about "shalom," it's time to pack your bags. We're going to the city of Cana!

Use a map or tablet to find Cana. Then mark both Bethlehem and Cana next to the correct dots on the map shown here.

How far is Cana from Bethlehem? Cana is

_____ miles

from Bethlehem.

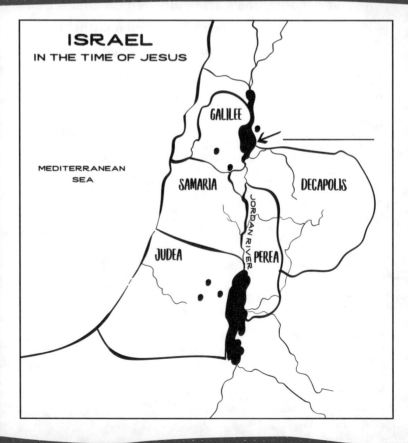

ISRAEL
IN THE TIME OF JESUS

GALILEE

MEDITERRANEAN
SEA

SAMARIA

DECAPOLIS

JORDAN RIVER

JUDEA

PEREA

Today, we're jumping from Jesus's small, ordinary birthplace to the town where He performed His first miracle. When I think of Jesus serving, I think of some amazing stories! People rising from the dead, blind men seeing, lame people walking, and demons being cast out of people. Those are incredible miracles. However, Jesus's first miracle was kind of ordinary. It didn't change any lives, and it wasn't a life-or-death situation.

KEEP THE PARTY ROCKIN'

Jesus and His disciples attended a wedding in Cana. Wedding parties lasted for days in Jesus's time. But something happened at this one to stop the party early. They ran out of wine. So, what's the big deal? It just means the party will be shortened a little, right? Read what happened next.

> "Three days later there was a wedding in the village of Cana in Galilee. Jesus' mother was there...Six stoneware water pots were there, used by the Jews for ritual washings. Each held twenty to thirty gallons. Jesus ordered the servants, 'Fill the pots with water.' And they filled them to the brim. 'Now fill your pitchers and take them to the host,' Jesus said, and they did.

> "When the host tasted the water that had become wine (he didn't know what had just happened, but the servants, of course, knew), he called out to the bridegroom, 'Everybody I know begins with their finest wines and after the guests have had their fill brings in the cheap stuff. But you've saved the best till now!'

> "This act in Cana of Galilee was the first sign Jesus gave, the first glimpse of his glory. And his disciples believed in him. John 2:1, 6-11 (MSG)

Why would Jesus pick this moment for His first miracle? Why a wedding? It's because He cares about the little things.

NOTHING IS TOO SMALL

Jesus wants to hear about both the problems and the victories in your life, even if they seem small. When you pray, you can bring anything to Jesus.

Some people say God doesn't really care how you feel as long as you are trying to be a better person, or more holy. That's not exactly true. Jesus wants you to feel:

- Content
- Safe
- Happy
- Balanced
- Healthy

In other words, Jesus wants to bring "shalom" into your life. In addition to being a greeting, shalom is a blessing of safety, happiness, contentment, balance, and wellness.

Jesus isn't only concerned about the times we are sick or sad. He serves us all the time, even in our happiest times. "But wait," you might ask. "What can Jesus do for me when I am having a great time? I've got all I need!"

Have you ever thought about why you are having a good time?

Things don't have to be a wreck for Jesus to serve you. Jesus cares about your happiness. He cares about the little things. In the same way, when you serve others in little ways, you're still showing love.

When you realize that Jesus wants you to have shalom in your life, you'll want others to have shalom too. That is one reason why you serve. Shalom is something people share together. It's about the whole group. We all win together.

Shalom!

CHALLENGE—LEMONADE AND COFFEE

Serve your neighborhood by doing a free lemonade or cider stand. If that's not possible, get a coffee gift card for someone as a present or treat the person behind you in line. Remember, Jesus values the little things that make us happy just as much as the big things.

RED ALERT!

In addition to turning water into wine in Cana, Jesus showed that he could heal from a distance when he was there. A royal official from Capernaum traveled to Cana, where he asked Jesus to come with him to heal his son. Jesus did heal his son—but He did it without even going to Capernaum!
(John 4:46-54)

DAY 22

JESUS GAVE COMFORT ON THE SEA OF GALILEE

WE'RE GOING TO THE SEASHORE!

Next stop—the Sea of Galilee!

Use a map or tablet to find the Sea of Galilee and mark it on the map below. Also, fill in the locations of Bethlehem and Cana. (Look back at Days 20 and 21 if you need a reminder.)

How far is the Sea of Galilee from Cana?

_____ miles

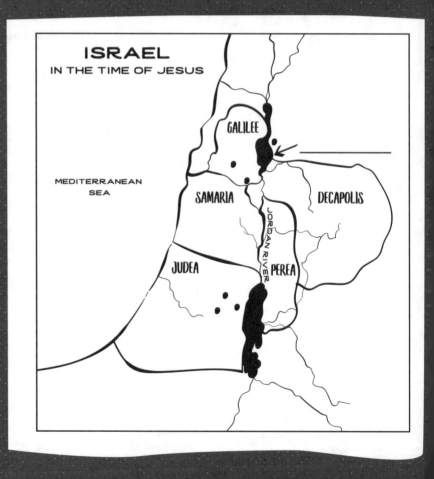

ISRAEL
IN THE TIME OF JESUS

MEDITERRANEAN SEA

GALILEE

SAMARIA

DECAPOLIS

JORDAN RIVER

JUDEA

PEREA

THE JESUS BOAT

Two fishermen, brothers Moshe and Yuval Lufan, trudged along the northwest shore of the Sea of Galilee—the same body of water where Jesus's disciples cast their nets. It was the winter of 1986, and drought gripped the region, causing the Sea of Galilee to lower.

Moshe and Yuval kept their eyes fixed on the muddy ground, wondering what they might find now that the water had lowered. Suddenly, they stumbled across what appeared to be a boat sunken in the mud along the edge of the Sea of Galilee.

They had come across an ancient fishing boat from the time of Jesus—one of the most remarkable discoveries in modern Israel. On the first day digging out the boat, the experts were amazed when a sudden downpour, lasting only about a minute, created a perfect double rainbow across the Sea of Galilee. One of the excavators said this was a sign from God, blessing the discovery.

You can see this boat in Israel today. It's called "the Jesus Boat" because it's just like the boat Jesus might have used. It also might be the kind of boat Jesus used when He got caught in a terrible storm.

THE STORMY 'SEA'

The Sea of Galilee is more like a big lake than a "sea." The writers of three gospels in the New Testament wrote about the same storm but in different words. On Day 14, we read the story from the point of view of Matthew. But today we're reading the same story from Mark's point of view.

After reading the Bible story below, glance back at Day 14 to see any differences between Matthew and Mark.

"Late that day he [Jesus] said to them, 'Let's go across to the other side.' They took him in the boat as he was. Other boats came along. A huge storm came up. Waves poured into the boat, threatening to sink it. And Jesus was in the stern, head on a pillow, sleeping! They roused him, saying, 'Teacher, is it nothing to you that we're going down?'

"Awake now, he told the wind to pipe down and said to the sea, 'Quiet! Settle down!' The wind ran out of breath; the sea became smooth as glass. Jesus reprimanded the disciples: 'Why are you such cowards? Don't you have any faith at all?'

"They were in absolute awe, staggered. 'Who is this, anyway?' they asked. 'Wind and sea at his beck and call!' Mark 4:35-41 (MSG)

Although Jesus was in the boat, the disciples were still scared when they saw the fierce wind and waves. Sometimes we pray for Jesus to be with us in hard times, but the disciples had Jesus with them, and yet they were still scared.

Jesus doesn't just promise to be with us, He promises to be in control of all things, even storms.

CALM IN THE STORM

Jesus will go with you wherever you are. No forest is so dark, no ocean so deep, no place too far away that His love can't reach.

During the storm, Jesus didn't just wring His hands, wondering what will happen. Instead, He was so relaxed that He slept soundly. Amazing! Jesus knows how everything will turn out. He wants us to have faith that He will take care of us the way He took care of the disciples. During the violent storm, Jesus calmed the waves and made the storm disappear.

Weather apps and meteorologists try to predict what the weather will be, but they cannot control the weather patterns. But Jesus can—and did. When Jesus calmed the wind and waves, the disciples realized how powerful He was. No one else could do that.

Big storms can be scary, especially when the power goes out or the sky gets dark. But no matter how big the storm that comes our way, we know God is in control of all things.

Even when things are dark, we can trust in God.

When you serve, things will not always go smoothly. It will be easy to get frustrated, tired, or even angry. But just remember, we can stay calm because Jesus is in control.

So, if you're scared, just imagine you're in the Jesus Boat. You can rest easy when He is the captain of your ship. Maybe you can even take a nap, as He did.

CHALLENGE—GIVE ME SHELTER

Some people lose everything in hurricanes, fires, or tornadoes. Do a scavenger hunt around the house. Use the list below to see how many things you can collect to give away. Once you have all your items, donate them to a local shelter or a rescue ministry.

Possible Items for a Family Donation Scavenger Hunt

- A shirt or t-shirt
- An accessory (belt, earrings, bracelet, ribbon, hat, scarf, etc.)
- A puzzle, game, or toy that is not broken or missing pieces
- 2 canned food items
- 1 boxed food item
- A book
- Sports equipment
- A DVD or CD
- A holiday decoration
- A pair of pants or shorts
- One item to donate of your choice!

For a real life photo of the Jesus Boat and to learn more about where Jesus walked, click on our free resources at:

WWW.SERVINGCHALLENGE.COM/FREE-KIDS-RESOURCES

RED ALERT!

The Jesus Boat was made from 12 types of wood, says the museum that houses it. One wood comes from a tree called Christ Thorn, a spiky wood that some believe was used to create the crown of thorns when Jesus was crucified. Another wood came from the Judas Tree, named after the disciple who betrayed Jesus. Those woods couldn't sink the Jesus Boat. Similarly, If Judas and the crucifixion couldn't sink the Kingdom of God, what can?

#SERVINGCHALLENGEKIDS

DAY 23

JESUS CONNECTED ACTION WITH COMPASSION IN NAIN

ON TO NAIN!

Next stop on the Israel Express is Nain. Use a map or tablet to find Nain and then mark it on the map. Also, fill in the locations of Bethlehem, Cana, and the Sea of Galilee (which you already found).

How far is Nain from the Sea of Galilee?

_____ miles

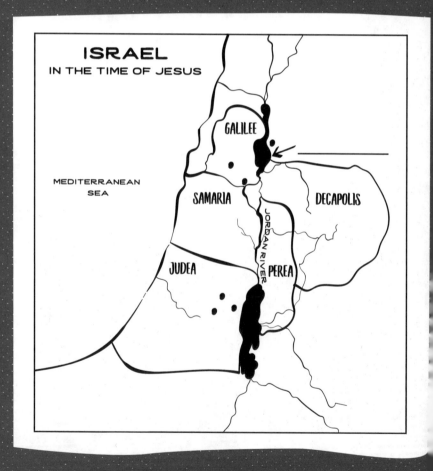

ISRAEL
IN THE TIME OF JESUS

MEDITERRANEAN SEA

GALILEE

SAMARIA

DECAPOLIS

JORDAN RIVER

JUDEA

PEREA

THE LEAF ROOF

Trees connect to other trees. You learned that tree roots are connected to fungi underground, creating an enormous, living web. Trees use this fungi web to share water, sugar, and nutrients. They also send signals of drought and warn other trees of dangerous insects.

However, trees don't use only their roots and fungi to connect. They also use their *branches* to stay in touch with one another. As trees grow, they stretch their branches until they overlap, creating a "roof." Trees will keep growing wider, reaching across empty space, until they feel the trees next to them. They try to fill in every gap. Once a branch touches another branch, it stops growing in that direction.

This roof of branches and leaves helps to keep the entire forest safe. It protects the forest from strong winds, creates a travel route for small animals to move around, and controls the temperature of the forest underneath.

The forest is healthiest when trees are connected. People are the same way. In the town of Nain, Jesus was surrounded by many people. But when He spotted a woman who was alone, He was heartbroken. Read about what happened in Luke's gospel below:

> **"Not long after that, Jesus went to the village of Nain. His disciples were with him, along with quite a large crowd. As they approached the village gate, they met a funeral procession—a woman's only son was being carried out for burial. And the mother was a widow. When Jesus saw her, his heart broke." Luke 7:11-13a (MSG)**

MATCHING COMPASSION WITH ACTION

As Luke writes, when Jesus saw the widow whose son had died, He was heartbroken. Another word for that feeling is "compassion."

Because the woman's husband had also died, she didn't have anyone else in her family. Women who did not have any family often became beggars or homeless, as they had no way to take care of themselves—unless they were cared for by the church or synagogue.

Jesus serves us because He sees our hurt. You don't have a single hurt that Jesus won't notice. When He sees us in pain, His heart breaks. Therefore, when we see others hurting, our heart should also break for them.

But the Bible tells us that Jesus didn't just feel sorry for her. He did something about it. Keep reading to find out what happened.

> "He [Jesus] said to her, 'Don't cry.' Then he went over and touched the coffin. The pallbearers stopped. He said, 'Young man, I tell you: Get up.' The dead son sat up and began talking. Jesus presented him to his mother.

> "They all realized they were in a place of holy mystery, that God was at work among them. They were quietly worshipful—and then noisily grateful, calling out among themselves, 'God is back, looking to the needs of his people!' The news of Jesus spread all through the country." Luke 7:13b-17 (MSG)

A LOT OF NERVE

Like an underground root network, you have a network of nerves working in your body. One of those, the vagus nerve, is the largest and one of the most important bundle of nerves. It runs from your brain down your neck and spine to all your organs. It controls the most important things like breathing or digestion.

Scientists discovered that the vagus nerve is also where compassion starts. They found that when you see suffering, your vagus nerve enables you to care. According to God's master design, caring for others is as important as breathing and eating.

But as Jesus showed, compassion isn't just about feeling and nerves triggering. Compassion is both feeling AND doing. Jesus was the perfect servant. He had compassionate feelings when He saw pain, but He also helped. When you notice someone's pain, you see them through Jesus's eyes. And when you jump into action, you show them Jesus's hands and feet. We are called to be the hands and feet of Jesus. When you match an action with a feeling, you are showing compassion as Jesus did.

Like trees reaching toward each other and like a church caring for its widows, we can create a safe place for everyone by reaching out to others. So, raise the roof with God's love today!

CHALLENGE—ACTION AND COMPASSION

Let's fire up that vagus nerve! Who is someone you know who may be hurting or struggling at school today? Keep an eye out for someone who might be sad. Can you match an action with your compassion?

DAY 24

JESUS FED THE HUNGRY IN BETHSAIDA

BETHSAIDA BOUND

Saddle up your donkeys. We're on our way to Bethsaida!

Use a map or tablet to find Bethsaida and mark it on the map below. Also, fill in the locations of Bethlehem, Cana, the Sea of Galilee, Nain, and Capernaum.

How far is Bethsaida from Nain?

_____ miles

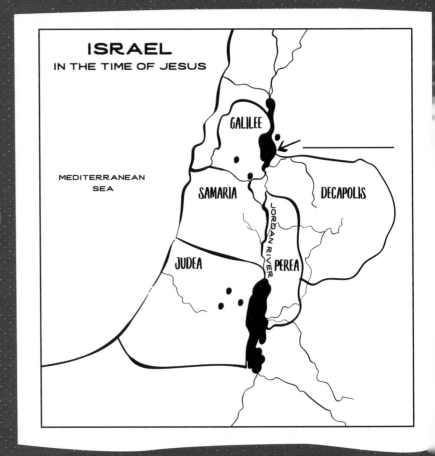

ISRAEL
IN THE TIME OF JESUS

GALILEE

MEDITERRANEAN SEA

SAMARIA

DECAPOLIS

JORDAN RIVER

JUDEA

PEREA

All this traveling makes me hungry! Draw your favorite snack in the picnic basket below.

Good thing you packed snacks because today you are learning that Jesus has power over our food! Today's story is so important that all four gospels—Matthew, Mark, Luke, and John—include it.

Jesus had been teaching people all day. In fact, the crowd was so focused on Jesus that no one planned anything for dinner. All they wanted was to hear more of what Jesus had to say. Read about what happened in the Bible story below.

"When Jesus landed and saw a large crowd, he had compassion on them, because they were like sheep without a shepherd. So he began teaching them many things.

"By this time it was late in the day, so his disciples came to him. 'This is a remote place,' they said, 'and it's already very late. Send the people away so that they can go to the surrounding countryside and villages and buy themselves something to eat.'

"But he answered, 'You give them something to eat.'

"They said to him, 'That would take more than half a year's wages! Are we to go and spend that much on bread and give it to them to eat?'

"'How many loaves do you have?' he asked. 'Go and see.'

"When they found out, they said, 'Five—and two fish.'

"Then Jesus directed them to have all the people sit down in groups on the green grass. So they sat down in groups of hundreds and fifties. Taking the five loaves and the two fish and looking up to heaven, he gave thanks and broke the loaves. Then he gave them to his disciples to distribute to the people. He also divided the two fish among them all. They all ate and were satisfied, and the disciples picked up twelve basketfuls of broken pieces of bread and fish. The number of the men who had eaten was five thousand." Mark 6:34-44 (NIV)

COMIN' RIGHT UP!

Have you ever been so hungry that you exclaimed, "I'm starving!"? If you did, you probably were not really starving. Starving means suffering or dying of hunger. It would take more than going a day without food to begin starving. You would need to go weeks and weeks with little food.

Sadly, not everyone has enough food to eat. There are 821.6 *million* people in the world who are starving right now. The food we throw out in America alone would be enough to feed millions of starving people. About 40 percent of our food in the U.S. is wasted. That means almost half of what we buy ends up in the trash.

It is estimated that 125 to 160 billion pounds of edible and nutritious food is thrown away in one year, according to the 2021 Global Hunger Index. The tricky part is finding a way to get that food to the people who need it. Many are working to solve this problem because no one should be dying of hunger.

One way you can help is to not say you are "starving" anymore. Even if you are just kidding around, it does not respect the millions of people who are starving in real life. Another way to help is to be less wasteful with your food. Let's reduce that 40-percent waste! Take smaller portions so you can finish your plate. Wrap leftovers and eat them later if you can't finish a meal at a restaurant. Also, eat at home and then use the money you saved to donate to your church food pantry.

Even Jesus wrapped up His leftovers! Jesus turned five loaves of bread and two fish into a meal for thousands. Afterward, the disciples picked up twelve baskets of leftover food. Jesus can use your small efforts to make a big difference!

CHALLENGE—WASTE WATCHERS

How much do you waste? Do a trash experiment. Keep an extra garbage can in the kitchen this week to put your scrap leftover food into. At the end of the week, see how much food you threw away. Make it a goal to reduce that food waste to zero!

DAY 25

JESUS BROUGHT HOPE IN BETHANY

HIKING TO BETHANY

I hope you're wearing your hiking shoes because now we're heading from Bethsaida to Bethany.

Use a map or tablet to find Bethany on the map below. Then fill in all of the locations so far, beginning with Bethany and moving on to Bethlehem, Cana, the Sea of Galilee, Nain, and Bethsaida.

How far is Bethany from Bethsaida?

_____ miles

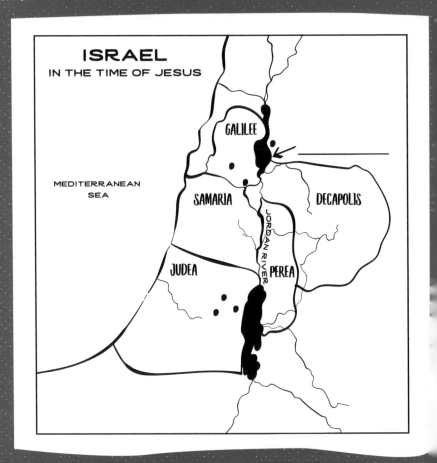

ISRAEL
IN THE TIME OF JESUS

GALILEE

MEDITERRANEAN
SEA

SAMARIA

DECAPOLIS

JORDAN RIVER

JUDEA

PEREA

BIG FEELINGS

We learned that trees can communicate with each other, but scientist Peter Wohlleben takes it one step further. He said, "Trees can feel pain, and they have emotions, such as fear. They like to stand close to each other and cuddle. Trees adore company and like to take things slow."

But not everyone agrees. Many other scientists say plants feel nothing at all. Emotions are for animals and people, which have nervous systems. You won't find nerves or brains in trees. For example, Professor Lincoln Taiz from the University of California Santa Cruz, said, "If the lower animals—which have nervous systems—lack consciousness, the chances that plants without nervous systems have consciousness are effectively nil." ("Nil" means "zero," as in zero chance.)

It's clear from Genesis that God set humans apart from animals and plants—and it's obvious from simple observation. As the famous writer G.K. Chesterton pointed out, birds have been building nests for a very long time. But what if birds suddenly started making more complex nests in different styles? What if they created nests like huge Gothic churches? What if birds wrote songs of praise or placed statues of other birds outside their "cathedrals." People would be astounded.

But birds remain birds. They're amazing and beautiful, but they're not like humans.

Humans are one-of-a kind. We're not just animals. We can build, create art, and do amazing things, like build computers and rocket ships. But we can also do terrible evil—more terrible than any bird or tree can do.

That's why it's so incredible that God became one of us. Jesus became human, and He felt our pains and sorrows. In Bethany, we see that Jesus had BIG feelings when he heard that His friend Lazarus died. All hope was lost.

WHEN THINGS GO FROM BAD TO WORSE

When Lazarus got sick, his sisters knew Jesus could heal him. So, they rushed to Jesus and told Him to come quickly to Bethany. They believed Lazarus could get well if their Lord just said the word. But instead of hurrying to them, Jesus took three days to reach Lazarus. He did not rush...

...and Lazarus died.

The women were heartbroken. When someone dies, it feels like the end of the world. The two women lost hope. But Jesus serves when things seem impossible.

When Jesus heard what happened to Lazarus, He began to cry and even yell in anger. Just imagine! God in Jesus was overcome with feelings over Lazarus's suffering. If Jesus were an average man, crying would be normal. But He is God.

Jesus knew He would raise Lazarus from the dead in just a few minutes. So, why didn't Jesus comfort the crying sisters right away? Why didn't He laugh it off or shrug His shoulders? Jesus cried because He loved Lazarus, Mary, and Martha.

Jesus will always come close to us when sad things happen.

GOD'S PLAN

It is not God's plan for us to go hungry like the 5,000 people in Bethsaida…or scared like the disciples in the tossing sea…or small and unimportant like the young mother Mary…or lonely like the woman who lost her son.

But death is not the end for Jesus. With God, all things will have a happy ending.

Jesus cries in disappointing moments, even when He knows things will work out okay in the end. He does this to "empathize" with us. "Empathy" is when we share the same feelings with someone.

We have a wonderful God who will be sad with us, but He won't leave us in our sadness forever. Read what Jesus said in Matthew. **"With man this is impossible, but with God all things are possible." Matthew 19:26b (NIV)**

Jesus called to Lazarus in the tomb: **"Lazarus, come out!"** He did the impossible for Lazarus, and He can do the impossible for you too! As James Hudson Taylor, a missionary to China in the 1800s, once said: "There are three stages to every great work of God. First, it is impossible, then it is difficult, then it is done."

CHALLENGE—IMPOSSIBLE DREAMS

What feels impossible in your life right now? This "impossible thing" might be someone sick or hungry in a faraway land or maybe in your town. How can you do one small thing for an impossible situation? Do something to help today.

"When I am afraid, I put my trust in you." Psalm 56:3 (NIV)

DAY 26

JESUS GAVE HIS LIFE IN JERUSALEM

LAST STOP: JERUSALEM!

Jesus finished His ministry in Jerusalem. So, it is only fitting that we end our tour of Israel in the Holy City— Jerusalem.

Use a map or tablet to find Jerusalem on the map below. Then mark it on the map, along with Bethlehem, Cana, the Sea of Galilee, Nain, Bethsaida, and Bethany.

How far is Jerusalem from Bethany?

_____ miles

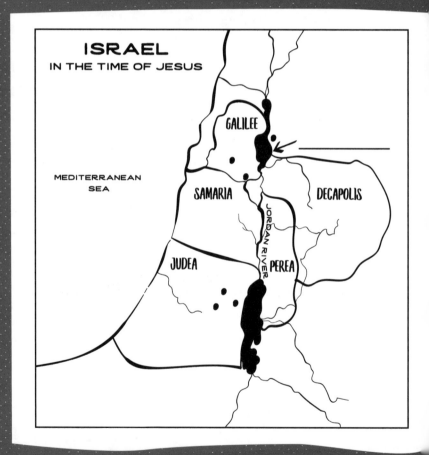

ISRAEL
IN THE TIME OF JESUS

GALILEE

MEDITERRANEAN SEA

SAMARIA

DECAPOLIS

JORDAN RIVER

JUDEA

PEREA

RUN FOR COVER!

According to *The Guinness Book of World Records*, the Manchineel tree, found in the Florida Everglades and the Caribbean, is the most dangerous tree in the world. All parts of the tree, including the fruit, are poisonous.

In fact, it's so bad that if you stood under the tree during a rainstorm, the water dripping off its apple-like fruit would leave terrible blisters on your skin. Just one single bite of the green fruit can give you severe pain and maybe kill you. And don't try to make a fire with that wood. The smoke from burning its branches causes blindness. Yikes!

We avoid dangerous things like the Manchineel tree, but Jesus was not afraid to face scary things. He faced the most dangerous tree of all—the wooden cross on which He died. (Because crosses are made from the wood of a tree, people sometimes say Jesus died "on a tree.")

Jesus faced His cross in Jerusalem, which means "City of Peace." But it was anything but peaceful for Jesus. In Jerusalem, the priests plotted to kill Him. Even though it was dangerous, Jesus did not stay away.

SEVEN TRIPS

Jesus went to Jerusalem seven times in His life. He was only eight days old the first time He went to the city, when Joseph and Mary brought Him to be dedicated at the Temple. The seventh and last time that Jesus went to Jerusalem was the week He died.

The prophet Zechariah predicted that Jerusalem would be a great city again. As he said, **"My cities will prosper again, God will comfort Zion again, Jerusalem will be back in my favor again." Zechariah 1:17b (MSG)**

When Jesus entered the city that seventh time, people were excited. They thought He was coming to defeat the Romans. By now, all the Jews in Jerusalem knew who He was, and they expected Him to finally claim the throne. Even the disciples thought Jesus was going to take over Jerusalem. Boy, would they be disappointed.

When Jesus came to Jerusalem, He made a grand entrance. He rode in on a donkey. This wasn't just a random decision. He was making good on all those promises about Him by the prophet Zechariah—prophecies highlighted in Matthew.

"Say to Daughter Zion, 'See, your king comes to you, gentle and riding on a donkey, and on a colt, the foal of a donkey.'" Matthew 21:5 (NIV)

The crowds threw palm branches and put blankets on the road before Jesus because they believed He was the Messiah. They sang in praise and celebration, **"Hosanna to the Son of David! Blessed is the one who comes in the name of the Lord! Hosanna in the highest heaven!" Matthew 21:9b (NIV)**

By choosing to enter Jerusalem on a donkey, not on a horse like a king, Jesus showed the people that He was humble. But the worst was yet to come.

ON THE CROSS

In Jerusalem, Jesus showed He was the greatest servant to ever live. He faced a tree way more dangerous than the Manchineel tree. He faced the cross of sin.

When the soldiers nailed Him to that wood, He wasn't just being killed. He was carrying all the sin and death of the world. One drop of that sin would be enough to kill us, but Jesus could take it.

By taking our sins to the cross, He did the greatest act of kindness we will ever see.

Today, Jerusalem is still a very important place. In Zechariah 1:17, we saw that the prophet predicted Jerusalem would be a great city again, and it became true. Millions of people travel to Israel every year to visit Jerusalem and see where Jesus lived. But Jesus is not in Jerusalem anymore. He is in heaven, and He lives in all our hearts.

So, remember, you don't need a passport to be with Jesus. You don't need to travel thousands of miles to meet Him. He's right there beside you. Listening. Waiting to be with you.

CHALLENGE—GOOGLE TRAVEL

Today, you can travel to the most distant places on the earth—places that earlier generations could only imagine. The internet is a powerful tool, which can be used in bad ways. But it is also a gift from God to do good.

It has been two thousand years since Jesus walked the earth. Some places look very different from what they looked like when He was there. Others look very much the same, like the Sea of Galilee. For more pictures of what Israel looks like today, go to our website at WWW.SERVINGCHALLENGE.COM/FREE-KIDS-RESOURCES

Use Google Earth to see what Jerusalem looks like today. If you have time, check out the other places we studied—Bethlehem, Cana, the Sea of Galilee, Nain, Bethsaida, and Bethany.

DAYS
27-33
OF THE 40-DAY
CHALLENGE

WHO DID SERVE?

JESUS

HAVE FUN COLORING THIS PAGE!
FIND MORE LIKE THIS AT SERVINGCHALLENGE.COM/FREE-KIDS-RESOURCES

THE FOREST OF REDVALE

PART 5

Emily ran to Red the Fox and threw herself into his arms. "I'm so sorry, Red! I'm so sorry!" She couldn't stop the tears from flowing.

Red gave her a gentle squeeze and said, "What's there to be sorry about? You and Isabella helped Aiden hold up the staff, which saved the day. The beetles are gone!"

Emily pulled away and wiped her eyes with the back of her hands. "But I caused the problem in the first place. I thought the beetle was lonely! I thought he needed help!"

"Wait, wait," said Red, putting a paw on her shoulder. "What are you talking about?"

As everyone gathered around, Emily launched into her story. She told how she left the path because she heard someone crying...how she met the beetle named Ed, who said he was lonely...how Ed asked her to get his drum down from the tree....and how the drum burst open on the ground, unleashing an army of bark beetles.

"It wasn't your fault. He tricked you," Isabella said. "You thought you were being compassionate."

Emily took a deep breath, for she hadn't told them the complete story. She was afraid to tell everyone she was jealous of Isabella for being so brave by healing the wounded tree with Living Water. She wanted people to see that she was the greatest servant of them all. That's why she rushed off the path to comfort the crying beetle, rather than wait for the others.

She was thinking more about herself than the beetle. If she had waited for Malachi, he probably would have known it was a trick.

"Isabella's right, Emily," said Aiden. "You were just being nice."

Aiden's actions with the beetles made her feel even worse. Sure, she helped hold up the staff. But Aiden was the one who had the idea of holding the staff up high in the first place. He was the True Servant! She was just a mess-up.

Malachi must have sensed there was more to her story because he tapped her on the arm and said, "Let's walk together."

So, Emily and Malachi stepped away and found a place to sit on a log. Malachi stirred the soil with the end of his staff. His amazing staff.

"Is there anything your staff can't do?" Emily asked.

"It can't make a good cheeseburger." Malachi grinned.

Emily laughed through her tears. "I'm so sorry about what happened," she said, rubbing her eyes again.

"I know you are. I can hear it in your voice. I can see it in your eyes."

"So, you agree that I have something to be sorry about? The others said I didn't...but I know they're wrong."

"I know you've been feeling bad about how this adventure has been going," he said, leaning closer and whispering. "I know you've been upset that back home, you've always been the one reaching out through your church, while Aiden runs off to basketball and Isabella stares at her phone."

Emily never understood how Malachi knew these things. But he had a way.

"It doesn't seem fair that when we come to Redvale, they're doing all of these incredible things, and I'm just messing up," she mumbled.

"Serving isn't about fairness. And it isn't about getting thanks for a job well done. I think you know that."

Emily shrugged. "I suppose you're right."

"When Jesus healed ten lepers of their terrible disease, only one returned to thank him," Malachi said. "That wasn't fair."

Emily had forgotten all about that story.

Malachi smiled. "Serving is not about us. It's about others."

"The crazy thing is that I should be happy that Isabella and Aiden are acting like heroes in Redvale. I should be thrilled they're finally serving."

"You've been a good example to them, Emily. Who knows? Maybe they wouldn't have acted like heroes in Redvale if they hadn't seen you do it back home."

"But what I do back home doesn't seem nearly as heroic as battling a fungus and beetles, like Isabella and Aiden did."

"I wouldn't be so sure. Doing good works may not be as dramatic as fighting monsters. But it's just as heroic."

Again, a shrug from Emily. "I suppose so."

Malachi nudged her. "All for one and one for all?"

"All for one and one for all," she said. She felt better. But only just a little bit.

THE VALLEY OF SHADOWS

When Malachi and Emily returned to the group, Isabella wrapped her little sister in a hug. "Are you feeling any better?"

Emily tried to smile, but Isabella could still see traces of tears in her eyes. "I am," she said, but not very convincingly.

"Thanks for helping me hold up that staff," said Aiden, strolling up to his sisters. "My arms were dying. I never could have done it if you two hadn't helped."

"But you were the one who thought of holding up the staff," Isabella pointed out. "How did the idea even come to you?"

"An image flashed in my mind of a man holding up a staff," he explained. "It was the most amazing thing."

Malachi got everyone's attention by thumping his staff on the ground. "All right, let's keep moving. We still have to plant those acorns before nightfall."

In all the excitement, Isabella had almost forgotten about the acorns. She checked her pocket to make sure it was still there. It was.

But a question still nagged at her. "Malachi, I get that we want to plant the acorns to save the oak trees. But I still don't understand…What about all the other trees dying in Redvale? How are we going to help them?"

"Excellent question!" Malachi said. "You're thinking like a True Servant, Isabella. Planting those acorns is only the first step toward rescuing the forest."

"So, what's the next step?" Aiden asked.

Malachi answered with a riddle. (He never made anything too easy.)

"Three strong staffs will rise from the light, and three brave trees will dine in the presence of the shadows," he said, his voice booming. "Then three hundred trees will clap their hands, and three thousand leaves will unfurl like flags."

Isabella, Aiden, and Emily exchanged confused looks.

"I don't get it," Aiden said.

"It's an old Redvale prophesy," Malachi said, "and I must admit I don't understand it fully myself. I only know that after we plant the seeds, we must go down into the Valley of Shadows."

Isabella's heart dropped. "The Valley of Shadows? That doesn't sound too safe."

"I've never been there before, so I really can't say. I only know that our path, the WAY, runs right through that valley."

It made Isabella a little nervous to think there were some things on this adventure that even Malachi didn't understand. But she trusted him.

So, they returned to the narrow path, winding through the forest. The air was clear and fresh, and the sky was a rich blue. Their path was ever upward—and tiring.

"How much farther?" Isabella asked a half hour later.

"Not far," Olive said. "Maybe another hour of walking."

That's not far? Isabella wondered.

In this part of the forest, the trees looked a bit healthier. Some of them even displayed the gorgeous colors of fall—brilliant reds, oranges, and yellows.

"The Destroyers haven't hit this part of the forest as hard," Jesse pointed out. "But if we don't stop them, these trees will soon start dying."

"This is one thing I miss living in Florida," Isabella said. "The trees at home don't change colors like this. The colors are more fabulous than I imagined."

As they continued, the trees began to thin out, and Malachi picked up the pace. It appeared they were reaching the very edge of the forest.

When they came out of the woods, they found themselves standing at the foot of a small hill. The sun sat low on the horizon, and soon it would be dark.

Malachi stopped and let out a deep sigh. Then he turned to the group and motioned toward the hill. "This is it. This is where you will plant your acorns. There's just enough light left in the day to get it done."

Isabella reached into her pocket and clutched her acorn, just to make sure it was still there. Suddenly, a wind roared from the forest, sending leaves swirling and twirling all around. Then a strange fog came creeping out of the forest and into the clearing.

Isabella shivered. Something told her this mission wasn't going to be easy.

FOG WOLVES

Aiden had seen this kind of fog before. When he and his two sisters came to Redvale the first time, he got lost in the forest, blinded by a dense fog. The fog was not like any he had ever seen before. It almost seemed alive, as it drifted from the forest and into the clearing where they stood.

"Hurry!" said Jesse. "Plant your acorns now!"

Olive nudged Aiden with a branch. "Plant them before they come!"

"Before who comes?" he asked.

"The wolves!" said Red.

Then Aiden remembered. During their first visit to Redvale, Malachi told them that wolves made of fog lived in the forest. He never saw the Fog Wolves, but he heard them. And now, he heard them again. An eerie howl rose from the forest.

That got Aiden moving. He and his sisters sprinted up the hill, moving as fast as they could. It wasn't a big hill, but it was steep enough to make the going slow. His legs burned.

By now, the fog became so thick that he lost sight of Jesse, Olive, Malachi, and Red. He could see only Isabella and Emily, but barely. They were on either side of him, only a couple of feet away.

"Malachi!" Isabella shouted. "Where are you!"

Suddenly, a brilliant light shone at the top of the hill, driving away some of the fog. The fog parted to the right and the left, creating a clear pathway up the hill. At the end of the path stood Malachi on top of the hill, holding up his staff. The tip of the staff glowed bright like a star.

"Light drives away the fog!" Malachi said, motioning them forward.

By the time they reached the top of the hill, Aiden was breathing hard. "What now?"

Malachi nodded to his right, where three golden shovels stuck from the ground, as if they had been waiting for them.

Emily snatched up one of the golden shovels and sank it into the soft, black soil. "How deep do we plant them?"

"In your world, acorns only need to be buried a few inches deep," came Red's voice, as the little fox appeared from the fog. "But in Redvale, acorns need to go deeper—about a foot."

The light from Malachi's staff was so strong that the fog retreated halfway down the hill. The air was clear at the very top, like a miniature mountain sticking from the clouds. They were soon joined by Jesse and Olive.

As Aiden dug into the ground, he heard the terrifying sound of wolves once again. Then he saw them. The Fog Wolves emerged from the fog, creeping up the hill slowly. There had to be at least a dozen of them. They were completely white, except for their bright orange eyes. Their bodies were not solid, for they were made from swirling fog.

But if Aiden recalled correctly, Malachi said they could still bite.

THE WAY

The ground was soft as Emily continued to dig. She kept her back to those horrible wolves, but she sensed them coming closer. The light of Malachi's staff was the only thing keeping them from pouncing.

"Please, Lord, keep your light burning," she prayed as she tossed a shovel-load of soil over her shoulder—and right into Red's face. By accident.

"Sorry," she said.

Red spluttered and spat out dirt. "No worries. Just keep digging as fast as you can."

Emily glanced over her shoulder, just for a second, and wished she hadn't. The number of Fog Wolves seemed to have doubled. So many glowing orange eyes. The growls were getting under her skin.

When Emily's hole was about a foot deep, she tossed aside her shovel and plucked the acorn from her pocket. Unlike acorns from their world, this Redvale acorn suddenly began to glow and felt warm.

"Quickly," said Isabella. "Plant it!" Her older sister was already covering her acorn with soil. Emily crouched and did the same, nestling the large acorn in the ground and scooping the soil back over it. She patted it down.

Their job was done, but the danger was still very much alive.

Standing back up, Emily turned to face the wolves. Several of them tried to edge closer, teeth bared. But every time one of them made a move, Malachi shone his light at them, and they scuttled backward.

Malachi's staff, with its glowing tip, was the only thing protecting them.

"Okay, what now?" Aiden asked.

"We need to protect those acorns through the night," Olive said.

"It's what Servanteers do," added Jesse.

Protect the acorns through the entire night? Emily's stomach twisted at the thought. "How are we going to keep the wolves away for that long?"

"I don't think it's possible," said Red, who usually looked on the bright side. If even he had given up, they were doomed.

"The wolves are going to increase in numbers," said Malachi. "And eventually, some of them are going to get past the light."

That didn't sound very encouraging.

Then Malachi gave Olive and Jesse the strangest look. He nodded his head, communicating without words.

"We can't let you do this," Jesse told Malachi.

"There must be another way," said Olive.

Emily felt a fear rise from her toes to her head. "What are you talking about? What can't you let him do?"

"We can't let him follow the WAY," said Red, as if that explained all.

"I don't understand," said Isabella. "What's the WAY?"

Olive didn't answer. She just sighed—a deep sigh that rustled all her leaves. Then Red began to cry. Emily had never seen Red cry before, and it terrified her. What was going on?

Malachi began to walk directly toward the Fog Wolves. The beasts kept their distance from the light, but they began to group together. Their howls became louder, and some of the Fog Wolves climbed over the others in their excitement.

Malachi stepped right into the swirling mass of fog. The Fog Wolves were all around him, only a few feet away, snarling and snapping. The light continued to keep them away, but it was beginning to dim, allowing the wolves to move closer.

Emily wanted to run to Malachi, to help him, but Olive extended a branch and held her back.

"Let me go!" Emily screamed. "His light is going out!"

"It's the WAY," said Jesse.

"What's the WAY? You've got to tell us!"

Red walked over and took her hand. "Whenever strangers spend the night in the Forest of Redvale, the wolves demand a payment."

"A payment? You mean money?" said Aiden.

"Wolves have no use for money," said Jesse. "They demand a life."

Emily tried to break away from Olive, but the tree used several more branches to hold her back.

Malachi's light was becoming ever dimmer, and the wolves were inches away from him by now, teeth bared. Emily put her hands over her ears to block the sound of their howls.

"But if he keeps his light bright, he can save himself," said Isabella. She too was beginning to sob.

"There is only one way out of this forest for all of us," said Jesse. "ONE WAY."

All at once, the light went out.

When the hill plunged into darkness, chaos erupted. Emily didn't think the howling could get any louder, but it did. She screamed. With the light doused, she could no longer tell what was happening to Malachi, but maybe it was good she couldn't see. The howling was awful enough.

Malachi didn't make a sound, so maybe the wolves weren't hurting him. Maybe he was using his staff to fight them off. He could do it if he wanted—although he told Aiden that his staff was for serving, not fighting.

But then a frightening thought slipped into Emily's mind. Maybe Malachi didn't want to fight off the wolves. Maybe he knew that their only way out of the forest was for him to let the wolves have their way with him.

Why did they ever come into this forest? Was it worth Malachi's life for them to plant these three trees? What if the Giant Birds returned and dug up the acorns? Then it would all be for nothing!

The sound of snarling wolves went on for what seemed like forever. Then, in an instant, in the twinkling of an eye, the howling ended. The ground buckled and shook, and Emily bolted for the spot where she last saw Malachi.

The fog slowly retreated into the woods, like waves pulling back into the sea. But there was no sign of Malachi—and no sign of the wolves. Their howls faded into the distance.

All that remained were three pieces of wood lying scattered on the ground. Emily picked one up, while Aiden and Isabella took hold of the other two.

It was Malachi's staff, shattered into three pieces. He was gone.

TO BE CONTINUED ON PAGE 210.

TO BE CONTINUED ON PAGE 210.

DAY 27

JESUS SERVES THE YOUNG

YES DAY

In the movie *Yes Day*, a group of parents agreed to say "Yes" to every request from their kids. And what a list they came up with!

Write out your own imaginary *Yes Day* list in the box below. Describe what you would like your parents to say "Yes" to.

A Yes Day might sound like fun, but it lasts only a day. What if your parents said "Yes" to you EVERY day? It sounds fantastic at first, but this experiment could quickly go bad. For example, what if you asked for all-day access to YouTube? What if you asked to eat whatever you want? What if you asked for unlimited money or no curfew?

If you did that every day, you would create some really bad habits. While it may seem unfair that parents don't allow you to do whatever you want, there are good reasons. It's kind of like trees…

SHELTERING LEAVES

When tiny seeds are planted and small shoots appear, you might think it would be good to spoil them with lots of sunshine and rainwater. But it is the opposite.

Older trees block 97 percent of the sunlight from reaching the shorter, younger trees. While that might seem to be a problem at first, it helps the little trees. Trees have the best chance of growing tall when they grow slowly. So, when the adult trees take a lot of the light from the little ones, they give them a better chance of a long life.

That doesn't mean the little trees—known as saplings—are left to fend for themselves. Because saplings don't get much sunlight, the full-grown trees help keep the little trees alive by sharing sap and nutrients with them.

To keep the baby trees healthy, the older trees must serve.

SHELTERING PARENTS

Like trees, children need to be protected by their parents, even from things that seem good. Friends, fun, and managing your own money sound great. But until we are strong enough for the responsibility that comes with these things, our parents or guardians need to keep us safe.

There are serious consequences when children are allowed too many freedoms. That's why Jesus issued strong warnings to those responsible for children:

> **"'If anyone causes one of these little ones—those who believe in me—to stumble, it would be better for them to have a large millstone hung around their neck and to be drowned in the depths of the sea. Woe to the world because of the things that cause people to stumble! Such things must come, but woe to the person through whom they come!'"**
> **Matthew 18:6–7 (NIV)**

YES, GOD

It's easy to think about all the things God says "No" to. But what are some things the Lord says "Yes" to?

He says yes to…

1 **OUR SAFETY**

"For you have delivered my soul from death, yes, my feet from falling, that I may walk before God in the light of life." Psalm 56:13 (ESV)

2 **OUR NEEDS**

"Yes, the Lord will give what is good, and our land will yield its increase." Psalm 85:12 (ESV)

③ COMING BACK TO US AGAIN

"He who testifies to these things says, 'Yes, I am coming soon.' Amen. Come, Lord Jesus." Revelation 22:20 (NIV)

You are Jesus's "Yes." He loves you so much that He went to the cross and died for you. Because Jesus said yes for you, you can give others your best yes!

CHALLENGE—YES!

Have a YES Day, but not exactly like the one in the movie. Instead, commit to saying yes to help those who ask.

For example...

- If Mom asks you to help her carry in groceries...say YES!
- If Dad asks you to take the dog for a walk...say YES!
- If your teammate asks if you can retrieve the ball at practice...say YES!

RED ALERT!

Sin entered the world when Adam and Eve ate fruit from the Tree of the Knowledge of Good and Evil. But a tree was also involved when sin was defeated on the cross by Jesus, who is sometimes called the Last Adam. In Acts 5:30, some translations of the Bible say Jesus was hung "on a tree" because the cross was made of wood from a tree.

DAY 28

JESUS SERVES
THE SICK

COVID CHAOS

The COVID-19 pandemic messed up a lot of lives across the planet—even the lives in your corner of the world. Did you miss school or wear a mask for a while? Did you or those in your family get COVID?

During the pandemic, a lot of people stopped going to church in person or participating in activities. Sports stopped. Movie theaters closed. Perhaps you did not see your grandparents for a very long time. In some doctor's offices, people still need to wear a mask today. COVID-19 turned the world upside down.

COVID-19 was like nothing we had seen before during our lives. But it wasn't the first time a pandemic happened, and it won't be the last.

Over a hundred years after Jesus died, in the year 165 AD, an even worse pandemic struck the world. For fifteen years, a sickness called smallpox killed one-third of the population of Rome.

Everyone in the land was terrified of smallpox. Many sick people were abandoned at home, while others fled from cities. No one understood the disease. The only way they knew to stop the sickness from spreading was to stay away from those who were already sick.

However, the Christians didn't flee the cities. Not only did they stay, but they took care of sick people. They didn't know much about nursing, but they did their best to keep sick people clean, fed, and hydrated. These basic things helped keep many people alive.

While they cared for the sick, they shared the love of Jesus with them.

Because Christians were around the sick, it strengthened their immune systems, so many never caught the disease—and if they did, they recovered quickly. Because of this, some people thought Christians were practicing magic. But the Christians knew that it wasn't their own powers that protected them. They insisted that God was healing people and protecting them.

Christianity grew and spread because these people were willing to serve the sick. Christians spread their love, which is a lot better than spreading germs.

HEALING AND SERVING

Sickness is not part of God's plan. It's a result of the Fall, which began in the Garden of Eden. But God still does miracles today, reversing the curse of sickness. God also heals by giving special gifts to doctors and the scientists who create medicines. But did you know that Christians started the first hospitals?

Because Jesus taught Christians to love and serve, His followers created hospitals because they believed these things:

1. God made everything perfect (at least in the beginning), so we should try to help people get well.

2. God made everyone equal, so every person should have a chance to be healed.

3. God wants us to love one another, and we can show that love by caring for those who are ill.

THE RED CROSS

The Red Cross is a famous medical organization that helps millions of people during floods and other disasters, armed conflicts, pandemics, and other health crises. And it all started in 1863 in Switzerland because of one man—Henry Dunant.

Henry helped wounded soldiers during a terrible battle in 1859. After the war, he worked with the government to take more action to protect war victims. Henry believed armies should care for all wounded soldiers, even the enemies. He also worked to get special help for the families of soldiers in the military.

Because of Henry Dunant's incredible work, the Red Cross helps more than two million people every year.

When you are sick, Jesus will be with you. When you cry out, He will always come to you. Jesus will use others to take care of you in the same way He used Christians to take care of sick people during the smallpox plague. As King David said when he cried to God, **"O Lord my God, I cried to you for help, and you have healed me." Psalm 30:2 (ESV)**

Like the Christians in 165 A.D. or Henry Dunant in 1859, you too can help others who are sick. You can make a difference. Jesus had compassion toward the sick, and He wants us to feel for those suffering as well. Even our vagus nerve (talked about on Day 23) tells us to feel compassion! When our hearts hurt for others, we have an opportunity to show them how much Jesus loves them.

CHALLENGE—PRAYER AND SERVICE

Below, write the names of sick people you know. Then pray that God heals them. Also, help someone who is sick today. Bring them a card or treat, send them a cheerful text, or give them a call. Offer to help them around the house because it may be hard for them to do everyday chores. We show Jesus's love when we serve those who are sick.

NAMES OF SICK PEOPLE WHO NEED PRAYER AND SERVICE

_____

_____

_____

_____

_____

RED ALERT!

The Book of Genesis mentions two trees. In addition to the Tree of the Knowledge of Good and Evil, there is the Tree of Life. After Adam and Eve sinned, they were cut off from the Tree of Life in the Garden of Eden. Death entered the world.

DAY 29

JESUS SERVES THE DISABLED

THE HEALING POOL

In the city of Jerusalem, a pool called Bethesda was believed to have magic powers. If you were the first to get in the pool after the water stirred, people thought you could become well.

For thirty-eight years, a man who hadn't been able to walk since birth laid by the pool, waiting to be healed. But unfortunately, he could never get to the water fast enough because no one would help him. Read about what happened.

"Now there is in Jerusalem near the Sheep Gate a pool, which in Aramaic is called Bethesda and which is surrounded by five covered colonnades. Here a great number of disabled people used to lie—the blind, the lame, the paralyzed. One who was there had been an invalid for thirty-eight years. When Jesus saw him lying there and learned that he had been in this condition for a long time, he asked him, 'Do you want to get well?'

"'Sir,' the invalid replied, 'I have no one to help me into the pool when the water is stirred. While I am trying to get in, someone else goes down ahead of me.'

"Then Jesus said to him, 'Get up! Pick up your mat and walk.' At once the man was cured; he picked up his mat and walked." John 5:2-9a (NIV)

God heals people through miracles, doctors, or medication. However, God sometimes takes what seems like a handicap and turns it into something extraordinary. A disability is an ability to help others in a unique way. This was true of Louis Braille.

BOOK-SMART

A small boy named Louis Braille was known for being very curious. His father owned a leather shop, and one day, when no one was around, Louis climbed up on the workbench and began using the tools. One tool poked his eye, which bled and became infected. The infection spread to his other eye, and soon Louis was completely blind. But because he was so young, he did not realize what was happening. He kept asking his parents why it was getting so dark.

When Louis was ten years old, he went to Paris to attend a special school for the blind. A soldier visited and showed the students a piece of paper with bumps. He explained that the dots and dashes on paper made it possible to send messages in the dark. Because the dots and dashes were raised up like bumps, the soldiers could use their fingers to read them without any light. (Although the system was created for soldiers, it was never used in the military.)

Louis realized this could be a way for the blind to read books. So, he made up his own system of dashes and dots for the alphabet. But the teachers at his school did not like the idea. They had their own teaching method and believed Louis was "too young" to change the system.

But Louis never forgot about his idea to help the blind read. After he became a teacher, he showed students how to read with his new system, and they loved it. They began telling others about the new way of reading, and soon blind people everywhere could read books on their own.

Louis's willingness to serve others who needed help changed the world. He had compassion for others and wanted things to be better. Today, the reading system for the blind is named after him: braille.

Louis was an organist at his church. Every Sunday, he would listen to God's messages about how Jesus healed people. Becoming blind was a tragedy, but God used it in Louis Braille's life to help thousands of other blind people. Louis did not give up when he was told that his blindness was a dead-end for reading. His faith helped him overcome his challenges.

CHALLENGE—ABLE TO HELP

Serve a disabled or handicapped person today. Below you will find a secret message written to you in Braille. Use a Braille alphabet found online to decipher the message.

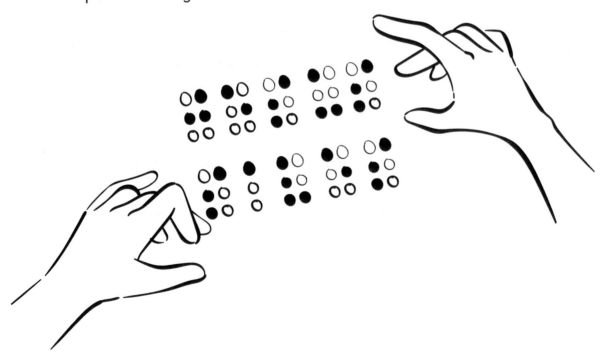

RED ALERT!

The Tree of Life, mentioned in the first book of the Bible (Genesis) also shows up in the final book (Revelation). In Revelation 22:2, the Bible says there will be a Tree of Life on either side of a river flowing from the throne of God. An eternal Eden will someday return.

#SERVINGCHALLENGEKIDS

DAY 30

JESUS SERVES ALL KINDS OF PEOPLE

AUTUMN COLORS

Decorate the tree below in fall colors.

For many people, their favorite part of Fall is the changing colors of leaves. But did you know those leaves don't actually change color? While it may look like green leaves suddenly become yellow, red, or orange, those colors were there all along. They were hidden underneath the green chlorophyll.

Chlorophyll is a chemical that helps trees make food. However, it is so strong that it covers up all the original colors of the leaves. As a result, we don't see the colors until the Fall when it gets too cold for chlorophyll.

We all have things that make us unique and beautiful, like the colors in leaves. But, like leaves, those differences are not always easy to see. They're hidden beneath the surface.

Some people say that to welcome differences, we should pretend we are all the same or look only for the things we have in common. But when we all try to look the same, talk the same, or wear the same things, our differences get hidden, like the vibrant colors under the chlorophyll.

TRUE COLORS

God wants us to be excited about our differences. There are over 60,000 tree species on the earth and between 11,500 and 13,000 distinct people groups.

Some people have big houses and multiple cars in their driveway, but most people in the world do not own a car. They have very little. Yet, underneath the skin, we are all children of God. That's why Jesus reached out to everyone—men and women, children and elderly, Jews and Gentiles, and rich and poor.

Take the case of the royal official from Capernaum. This man was very rich, but his money could not save his son. Here is what happened:

"And there was a certain royal official whose son lay sick at Capernaum. When this man heard that Jesus had arrived in Galilee from Judea, he went to him and begged him to come and heal his son, who was close to death.

"'Unless you people see signs and wonders,' Jesus told him, 'you will never believe.'

The royal official said, "Sir, come down before my child dies."

"'Go,' Jesus replied, 'your son will live.'

"The man took Jesus at his word and departed. While he was still on the way, his servants met him with the news that his boy was living. When he inquired as to the time when his son got better, they said to him, 'Yesterday, at one in the afternoon, the fever left him.'

"Then the father realized that this was the exact time at which Jesus had said to him, 'Your son will live.' So he and his whole household believed."
John 4:46b-53 (NIV)

Jesus healed the royal official's son without even being there. It didn't matter to Jesus that this man was royalty or had lots of money. Money can't fix every problem. Only God's riches—only His love and grace—can do that.

REACHING OUT

Trees with deep, healthy roots grow wide branches that reach out, gathering all the sunshine they need. In forests, branches stretch so far that they overlap with branches of nearby trees. This is what Jesus did. He reached out. He stretched out His arms, like branches, and touched everyone with His mercy.

Because Jesus had deep roots, He could reach out and love those who were different from Him—without changing His beliefs. We don't have to change who we are to serve people who are different. We can still be sure of what we believe and how we show our faithfulness to God. Those are things we will never change.

If we have deep roots, if we know what we believe, we can grow wide branches that reach out to others who are different. Maybe we'll even learn that we have some things in common with them. Maybe we overlap like the branches of trees in a forest.

Even when we are not the same, we can work together. In fact, the stronger we are in our habits with God, the better we will be in reaching out to others. (For more on habits with God, check out *Being Challenge Kids* at WWW. REDLETTERCHALLENGE.COM.)

You cannot change what you look like, your family, or your life story. They are a part of who you are. Let your uniqueness shine through like the colors of Fall leaves. When you reach out to serve and love others, your differences make you as beautiful as a blazing red tree at the height of autumn.

CHALLENGE—MAKE A DIFFERENCE

Talk to someone from a different generation than you. Being born in another time gives you a point-of-view that you may not have ever seen before.

DAY 31

JESUS SERVES ALL NATIONS

QUIZ TIME!

Try to match the question with answers from the list below:

ANSWERS:

THE UNITED STATES AND THE FLAG

FOUR

WASHINGTON, D.C.

PRESIDENT

GEORGE WASHINGTON

CONGRESS (LEGISLATIVE), PRESIDENT (EXECUTIVE), THE COURTS (JUDICIAL)

EIGHTEEN AND OLDER

NOVEMBER

DEMOCRAT AND REPUBLICAN

QUESTIONS:

1. Who was the first president?

2. Name **one** branch or part of the U.S. government?

3. How old do citizens have to be to vote for president?

4. How many years is the US president elected for?

5. In what month do we vote for president?

6. What is the capital of the United States?

7. Who vetoes bills?

8. What are the **two** major political parties in the United States?

9. What do we show loyalty to when we say the Pledge of Allegiance?

Answer Key on page 198

These are only nine of the 100 questions that immigrants to America must answer to become citizens. Immigrants are people who permanently move to a foreign country. Here are some facts about immigrants:

- The United States has a larger immigrant population than any other country.

- In 2015, the United States had 47 million immigrants.

- 17 percent of the medical workforce in America are immigrants.

- One out of every four workers in retirement homes are immigrants.

Not only must immigrants take the citizenship test, but they need money to pay for it. Today, it costs $725 per person to become a U.S. citizen, but many immigrants do not have the time to study or the money to pay for the test. Therefore, a 78-year-old woman, Rita Siebenaler, decided to help.

The workers in Rita's retirement home were immigrants from Cameroon, Haiti, or Jamaica, so Rita asked if the residents living there would help. According to the *Washington Post*, the residents "tutored the health aides, housekeepers and cooks, drilling them on spelling, the constitutional amendments, the writers of the Federalist papers, the rights of U.S. citizens and other questions on the citizenship test that a huge percentage of American-born citizens who call themselves patriots would flunk."

This is a wonderful story because immigrants are not always treated kindly. From the beginning, God taught His people to share and help each other. At Rita's retirement home, the immigrants helped residents with things they couldn't do any more like cooking, cleaning, and driving. The residents, in turn, helped the immigrants get citizenship. They also raised $40,000 to pay for their tests and quizzed them on the questions while they worked.

All their efforts paid off. So far, the residents have helped almost ninety immigrants become American citizens.

A ROMAN CAPTAIN'S REQUEST

Helping people of other cultures was also important to Jesus. He was a Jewish man, and He primarily served the Jews. But He still loved and served all people from all cultures. He even helped a Roman captain.

"As Jesus entered the village of Capernaum, a Roman captain came up in a panic and said, 'Master, my servant is sick. He can't walk. He's in terrible pain.'

"Jesus said, 'I'll come and heal him.'

"'Oh, no,' said the captain. 'I don't want to put you to all that trouble. Just give the order and my servant will be fine. I'm a man who takes orders and gives orders. I tell one soldier, "Go," and he goes; to another, "Come," and he comes; to my slave, "Do this," and he does it.' Matthew 8:5-10 (MSG)

"Then Jesus turned to the captain and said, 'Go. What you believed could happen has happened.' At that moment his servant became well." Matthew 8:13 (MSG)

Roman soldiers were known for being rough and mean, so many people were afraid of them. But Jesus served them anyway.

We too can show love to others who come from different cultures. It is natural to want to spend time with people who are similar to you, but it's also important to find ways to care for people who are different. You don't have to be a certain race or people group to be in God's family!

CHALLENGE—HELPING IMMIGRANTS

Find out what organizations exist in your town or state to help immigrants. Donate or research how you can help an immigrant today.

RED ALERT!

If you go to Capernaum today, you can see what is believed to be the remains of Peter's house. Jesus made Capernaum the headquarters for His ministry because a lot of people passed through this town. Matthew collected taxes on the busy trade route through Capernaum.

DAY 32

JESUS SERVES HIS ENEMIES

ATTACK ON PEARL HARBOR

On December 7, 1941, the Japanese bombed Pearl Harbor, bringing America into World War II. However, many people do not realize that the very next day the Japanese also attacked the Philippines.

December 8, 1941, changed everything for fifteen-year-old Felipe Merioles, who lived in the Philippines. When the Japanese soldiers invaded, Felipe vowed to protect his sisters and pregnant sister-in-law. One day, a lost Japanese soldier came to their home and demanded directions. Rather than showing him the correct way, Felipe took a machete and led the soldier deep into the woods, where he killed the man when his back was turned.

Filipe joined the army as a messenger and would often have to hide from Japanese soldiers in tall grass. As he hid, not moving a muscle, ants would bite him. He could see nearby fruit to eat, but if he reached for it, he would risk being spotted. So, he lay as still as a mouse, hungry and thirsty for hours and hours. If he had to use the bathroom, he would have to go in his pants. If he had moved in any way, he would have been killed.

Felipe hated the Japanese.

THE ESCAPE

When the fighting got too close, Felipe and his family decided to escape. The journey was too hard for Felipe's pregnant sister-in-law, who died while delivering her baby on a tree stump. The baby died too, and Felipe wondered if everyone he loved would die. He felt hopeless.

After the war, Felipe met a missionary who taught him about Jesus. He went to Bible college and studied to be a pastor. One day, a missionary brought special guests to church. They were former Japanese soldiers who had become Christians. At first, no one spoke. It was very quiet. Then, one at a time, the soldiers stood up and told their stories. Felipe realized that the Japanese men had not wanted to hurt him. They were following orders.

Felipe was finally able to forgive them. At the end of the service, bowls and towels were brought out. First, the Japanese soldiers washed Felipe's feet, and then Felipe washed theirs. It was a powerful experience. To remember that day, Felipe asked one of the special guests to sign his Bible. He signed in both Japanese and English. This is what he wrote:

CAPT. MITSUO FACHIDA—THE OFFICER WHO LED THE ATTACK ON PEARL HARBOR ON DEC 7, 1941.

LUKE 24:34 "FATHER, FORGIVE THEM, FOR THEY KNOW NOT WHAT THEY DO...."

Jesus said those exact words of forgiveness as He died on the cross. Most of Jesus's friends had abandoned Him, too afraid of being caught by the Romans. So, when Jesus went to the cross to die, He was alone, except for several women who had followed Him.

In a way, everyone became Jesus's enemy because He died for all of our sins. All of us were responsible for His death. That includes you and me.

> **"For if while we were enemies we were reconciled to God by the death of his Son, much more, now that we are reconciled, shall we be saved by his life." Romans 5:10 (ESV)**

As a pastor, Felipe was dedicated to serving others and telling them about Jesus. Whenever he opened his Bible, the signature of his enemy was right there, reminding him that Jesus was a servant and died for everyone, even our worst enemies.

CHALLENGE—LOVE YOUR ENEMIES

Pray for your enemies today. It could be a bully at school, a company doing shady business, or terrorists fighting against our country.

RED ALERT!

King David made Jerusalem the capital of the Jewish kingdom somewhere around 1,000 BC. Since then, it has been ruled by Romans, Persians, Arabs, Fatimids, Turks, Crusaders, Egyptians, Mamelukes, and Muslims. Today, Jerusalem is sacred to three major religions—Judaism, Christianity, and Islam.

#SERVINGCHALLENGEKIDS

DAY 33

JESUS IS OUR SERVANT KING

TRADING PLACES

If you could trade places with one of these people for a day, who would you choose?

- The president
- A rich businessman
- A YouTuber (influencer)
- A famous athlete
- A world-class musician
- A cake-taster

Or [_____] (Make up your own!)

KING OF THE CLASSROOM

A teacher thought it would be fun for her students to have a taste of sitting in the teacher's seat, so she invented a reward called "King of the Day." In her classroom, students could earn the right to switch seats with the teacher for an entire day. (She remained the teacher, but she couldn't use her chair or desk.) The teacher would trade places, sitting in the student's small plastic chair and using their cramped desk, while the student would have an adjustable leather chair that rolls and reclines. What a fantastic way to spend the day! It might even make doing homework fun! (Okay, maybe not.)

This week, you learned that Jesus served all kinds of people. He served the young, sick, disabled, different races and people groups, the wealthy and poor, and He even served His enemies. Jesus served all people, including you.

When people serve us, we might be tempted to think that makes us their master. So, we lift ourselves up, even above Jesus. We begin to order Him around, telling Him what to do, when to come, and where to go. We think we know best.

God did not become your servant so we could boss Him around. He will not be told what to do. God is not an expert we can Google when we feel like it, nor is He a buddy we use when we are bored. God became our servant so we can join Him in servanthood. Read this verse below.

> **"To you, O God, belong the greatness and the might,**
> **the glory, the victory, the majesty, the splendor;**
> **YES! Everything in heaven, everything on earth;**
> **the kingdom is all yours! You've raised yourself high over all.**
> **Riches and glory come from you. You're ruler over all."**
> **1 Chronicles 29:11-12 (MSG)**

If all that is true about our mighty God, then He must know much better than you how everything works. You do not want Him to grant all our wishes all the time because sometimes you can be wrong. But God knows what to do, and He will do what is best. The moment we look up to God, we take the place of a servant.

SERVING, POWER, AND MAJESTY

On Day 15, we talked about how Jesus gave us an example of how to serve by washing His disciples' feet. His serving didn't take away His power and majesty. Jesus was a Servant King. Here is what Jesus said after He washed His disciples' feet.

"Do you understand what I have done to you? You address me as 'Teacher' and 'Master,' and rightly so, This is what I am. So if I, the Master and Teacher, washed your feet, you must now wash each other's feet. I've laid down a pattern for you. What I've done, you do." **John 13:12-14 (MSG)**

Just because the teacher gave up her seat, it did not take away her authority in the classroom. Similarly, just because God serves you, that does not mean God is not your Lord.

When we serve others, we bring glory to God. It is easy to look at others and try to decide if they deserve help or not, but when we do everything to give glory to Jesus, it doesn't matter if the person deserves it or not. God gets the glory!

CHALLENGE—KINGS AND QUEENS

Ask someone, "If you could be king or queen for a day, what would you do?" Listen to their response and try to do one thing to make them feel important today.

RED ALERT!

One of the most famous streets in Jerusalem today is known as the Via Dolorosa, or "The Way of Sorrows." This is the route that tradition says Jesus followed, carrying His cross through the streets of Jerusalem. He eventually wound up at the "place of the skull"— Golgotha. That's where Jesus, our Servant King, was crucified.

#SERVINGCHALLENGEKIDS

WHAT DI

DO BY S

D JESUS

ERVING?

THE FOREST OF REDVALE

PART 6

The Fog Wolves were gone, but so was Malachi.

Night had fallen, and a full moon cast an eerie light on the hill. The forest surrounding the clearing had returned to the normal sounds of insects and owls. It was peaceful, as if nothing terrible had happened.

Isabella still couldn't believe that Malachi didn't fight back when the Fog Wolves pounced on him. She forced herself to ask Olive the question she feared most.

"What happened to Malachi? Is he dead?"

Olive leaned over, her branches drooping. "He sacrificed himself," she said. "He knew that someone had to give themselves to the wolves."

Isabella wiped a tear from her cheek. "But there had to be another way."

"There wasn't," said Jesse, his eyes downcast.

The three Perez children still held the three pieces of Malachi's broken staff in their hands. Looking down at her piece, Isabella wandered over to where they had planted the three acorns on the hill. Then she drove the broken staff into the ground where she had placed her acorn. Emily and Aiden did the same.

"Why couldn't one of us make the sacrifice?" asked Emily, sitting down on the grassy slope.

"This is the way it had to happen," said Red. "Malachi sacrificed himself to show you the path of servanthood. He was called to lead. You are called to follow."

"But follow where? We're lost in these woods without him," Aiden said.

"Don't worry," said Olive. "There is still a way out of the woods. For now, our duty is to stay here and guard the acorns you just planted. As long as we stand guard, no harm will come to the acorns."

Isabella ran a hand through her hair. "But it takes a long time for an acorn to grow. We can't stay here forever!"

"No, but you can stay here one night." Olive patted Isabella on the head. "Get some rest. Go to sleep."

How can I sleep at a time like this? Isabella thought.

Suddenly, a wind rustled the leaves all around them, as if the forest were alive and the trees were talking. Then an overwhelming sleepiness swept over Isabella, and her eyes felt heavy. She tried to keep her eyes open, but it was a losing battle.

Darkness came down like a soft, warm blanket being tucked around her by her parents.

●　●　●

When Isabella opened her eyes, the sun was shining brightly. She looked up and found Red staring down at her and grinning. It was the morning of a new day.

Why was Red smiling after the worst night of their lives? Isabella raised herself into a sitting position and looked around. She found herself staring at the thin trunk of a four-foot-high tree. That wasn't there when she went to sleep!

Three trees stood where they had planted the three acorns and the three pieces of Malachi's staff the night before.

Isabella rubbed her eyes. "What? That's not possible. Trees don't grow this tall overnight!"

"These trees do," said Red, hopping around in delight.

"I can't believe it either, sis." Aiden ran a hand down the bark of the young tree. "But the proof is right here before us."

Isabella grinned. Despite her deep sadness, there was something about the three young trees that brought her joy.

The only person not smiling was gruff old Jesse. He stomped toward them from the woods, carrying three golden objects, flashing in the sunlight.

When he reached the top of the hill, he tossed the objects at the feet of the three Perez kids. Isabella looked down at them in horror. They were axes! Three golden axes!

"It's time," Jesse said. "It's time to cut down the three trees."

THE THREE AXES

Aiden exploded. "What do you mean it's time to cut down these trees? We just planted them! And Malachi sacrificed his life so we could do that! Sorry, I'm not cutting them down!"

"Stop being so stubborn," scolded Jesse, but Olive took the gentle approach.

"It's not your choice," she said softly. "These three trees have chosen to sacrifice themselves. They chose to serve, and you can't deny them that."

Aiden waved his arms. "But what good is cutting them down? I don't get it."

"Malachi was cut down by the wolves, and his sacrifice saved your lives," said Olive.

"But that's different!" shouted Emily. "I don't see the purpose of cutting down the trees we fought so hard to plant!"

Olive looked up at the sky and sighed. "I wish I could tell you I knew the reason. I only know there is a purpose behind it all."

"It's the WAY," said Jesse, pushing a shovel into Aiden's hands. "You don't always know the WHY when you're following the WAY."

Aiden stared at the golden axe in his hands. Then he looked at the trees, these miraculous trees that had grown overnight.

For some strange reason, he thought about playing basketball. He thought about how his coach creates plays, and sometimes they don't make any sense. But even when Aiden doesn't think a play will work, he does it anyway because his job is to follow the coach's directions.

And most times, to his surprise, the play works marvelously, even when he least expects it.

"Malachi would want you to do it," Olive said.

"Then I wish he would've told us," said Isabella.

"Okay, I'll do it," Aiden mumbled. "It seems crazy, but if Malachi wanted us to cut down the trees, I'll do it."

"No!" shouted Emily.

As Aiden moved toward the tree on the right, Emily tried to stop him.

"Step aside, Emily. Give me room."

"Give him room, give him room!" commanded Jesse, nudging Emily out of the way.

Aiden had cut down trees a few times in his life—on Christmas, when his parents took him to a tree farm. But he used a saw then, not an axe. This would be the first time he ever wielded an axe.

Swinging with all his power, the blade went through the trunk of the tree smoothly and cleanly. It was almost like slicing air. The tree remained standing for a split second before tumbling over. It hit the ground with a loud thud—which is very strange for such a small tree.

Then a brilliant flash burst from the ground, blinding Aiden and forcing him to close his eyes. When he opened them again, he couldn't believe what he was looking at.

THE THREE STAFFS

Aiden's tree turned into a staff when it hit the ground!

After the burst of white light, like lightning from the ground, Isabella opened her eyes. The tree that Aiden cut down had become a walking stick, just like the one Malachi carried, only smaller.

Eagerly, Isabella lifted her axe. She wasn't athletic like Aiden or Emily, so she wondered whether she was strong enough to chop down the second tree. But it was easier than imagined.

This time, Isabella shielded her eyes from the explosion of light when her tree fell to the ground. And when she opened them? Another staff.

Emily, who had opposed the idea, was the next to go. Another slice. Another blast of light. Another staff.

Three trees had become three staffs for three very surprised kids.

"I didn't see *that* coming!" exclaimed Jesse.

Red danced around in excitement.

"Your rod and your staff, they comfort me," said Olive, solemnly.

Those words sounded familiar to Isabella. She thought it was one of the Psalms of David. Something about how God's staff gives us comfort even in the darkest of times.

The old tree leaned over, creaking with age. She said, "Three strong staffs will rise from the light, and three brave trees will dine in the presence of the shadows. Then three hundred trees will clap their hands, and three thousand leaves will unfurl like flags."

Isabella stared at the staff in her hands. "The beginning of that Redvale prophecy now makes sense: Three strong staffs will rise from the light. But I still don't get the other part."

"Yeah," said Aiden. "What's all that about three brave trees dining in the presence of shadows?"

"I can't say I know for sure," said Jesse, "but I think you are the three brave trees. And I think you must carry these staffs to the Valley of Shadows."

"In the valley, you must have a meal surrounded by your enemies. That will bring the forest back to life," added Olive.

A coldness crawled up Isabella's back at the mention of the name "Valley of Shadows."

"This is exciting!" shouted Red, laughing. "Which way to the Valley of Shadows?"

"You act like we're going to a playground," said Aiden. "It sounds dangerous."

"It is dangerous!" said Red. "But don't you remember the Psalm from the Bible? It says God's rod and staff will comfort you in the Valley of Death! God carries a staff and a rod, just like a shepherd does. And you know what a shepherd does with his staff? He uses it to drive away wolves and protect sheep! God will do the same. He'll protect you! You're His sheep!"

Isabella looked once again at her staff, a simple, slender thing. Was this God's staff? Could something so fragile be so strong? Will it really protect her?

"We've been babbling long enough," said Jesse. "There is no time to lose! We must make haste to the Valley of Shadows before the day is over!"

"We are Servanteers!" shouted Red. "And Servanteers serve, even when they're afraid!"

"All for one and one for all," said Isabella nervously. Although she wanted to be home on her couch, curled up with her phone, she knew this mission was far more important than anything she could watch on a screen.

She stepped before Olive. "Lead the way."

The old tree gazed down on her and smiled. "Your heartwood continues to get stronger, seedling." Then the olive tree turned and walked back into the forest.

The others followed, disappearing into the trees and marching toward the Valley of Shadows.

THE ROOT OF JESSE

Whenever Emily kept her hand curled around her wooden staff, she felt strong. She sensed the power of an oak seeping through her hand, keeping the fear away. She felt more alive, more excited than she could ever remember.

As they wound their way past a gurgling stream, Emily noticed a strange thing about Jesse. A small stem with a single leaf shot out from the top of the stump's flat head. She hadn't noticed that before.

"Don't look now, Jesse, but something's growing from your head," she said.

Jesse shot his eyes upward. "There's something on my head? I thought I felt something up there growing."

"So...stumps can still grow?" Emily wondered.

"Of course! Do I look dead?" The tree stump sounded miffed by the question.

"No, no, no. It's just that...I thought tree stumps were..."

"You thought stumps can't grow!" Jesse exclaimed, before softening his voice. "It's a common mistake. But some tree stumps can regrow, especially if they have strong roots. And olive trees have very strong roots. We're well-known for growing back when people think we're goners. But it's all about the roots!"

Emily studied Jesse, who hiked along on stubby legs. "Where are your roots? I can't see them."

"Trees like me and Olive do have roots, but they can't be seen. And strong roots mean a strong and long life. Olive trees can live thousands of years because we regrow, even when people think we're dead."

"I'm sorry. I should've known," said Emily.

Then grumpy old Jesse laughed. It was the first time she heard him chuckle. "I bet you also don't know that people have roots too!"

Now, it was Emily's turn to laugh. "People don't have roots. We have legs, not roots."

"Like me, your roots can't be seen. But if your roots are deep, if your roots are connected to God, you'll live long and strong. In fact, you'll live forever!"

"We're almost there," said Olive.

Emily had been so busy talking that she wasn't paying attention to the growing darkness. The forest had become thick, with very little light reaching the ground. Her heart began to thump wildly.

"Follow me," said Olive. She led them down a narrow path, leading to the edge of a steep cliff, and they looked down on a valley filled with trees. Most of the trees appeared completely dead. No leaves at all. Their bodies were nothing but dead wood. Skeletons really.

"Welcome to the Valley of Shadows!" said Red excitedly.

A dark shadow draped across the entire valley like a great stain. The only part of the valley not covered in shadow was an enormous tree. It stood in the heart of the valley in a circle of light.

"That is the Tree of Life," said Olive.

Emily gripped her staff more firmly. "I will fear no evil, for you are with me. Your rod and your staff comfort me." She prayed those words over and over. Then Olive led them down a narrow path leading into the valley. Emily trembled at the thought of what lay ahead.

SHADOW WOLVES

Aiden had never seen so many dead trees with leafless branches reaching out at them like skinny fingers. He tried to keep his eyes on the path ahead, which plunged into the valley.

As the darkness deepened, a light suddenly lit up the tip of his staff. The same thing happened to Emily and Isabella's staffs. The three staffs, with three lights, wrapped them in a comforting glow. Soon, it was as dark as night, even though it was the middle of the day.

Because of the recent rain, the path was muddy. Aiden nearly slipped several times, and so did his sisters. It was tough going.

Then things began to move in the shadows all around them.

"Don't look at the Shadow Wolves," said Olive. "Keep your eyes on the Tree of Life."

Shadow Wolves? First, they faced Fog Wolves and now Shadow Wolves? Aiden thought they were done with these creatures.

"The light shines in the darkness, and the darkness has not overcome it," Isabella said.

Aiden knew those words were Scripture, but he didn't know which book or verse. He wasn't good at memorizing like Isabella. But he liked the message of the words.

"The light shines in the darkness, and the darkness has not overcome it," he repeated.

The light of their staffs kept the wolves from getting too close. But every so often, one of the beasts braved the light and moved into their circle of brightness. Then Jesse would snarl at them, and the wolf would scuttle backward, whimpering like a dog.

Stumps snarl? Jesse was full of surprises.

When they reached the bottom of the valley, they came to the Tree of Life. This was the only tree for miles that still looked alive—which made sense because it was called, after all, the Tree of Life. Its leaves were green and flourishing.

"There's a treehouse!" Aiden exclaimed. He loved treehouses, and this tree had a beautiful one, nestled in its branches. A circular staircase led up the side of the large tree.

"Can we go inside?" he asked.

Olive nodded. "Of course you may. I believe a meal is waiting for you."

"But you're too big to fit in the treehouse," Emily pointed out to Olive.

"Don't worry about us," she said. "Jesse and I will stay down below while you eat."

"But what about the Shadow Wolves?" Aiden was afraid that Olive and Jesse would be attacked without light to drive the beasts away. "Here, let me give you my staff as light."

Jesse barked in anger. "No! You must hold on to your staff! It's the WAY it should be."

"But it was a kind thought, Aiden," said Olive gently. "Thank you."

"Yes, it was a kind thought," said Jesse, calming down.

With their staffs in hand, Aiden led the way up the spiral staircase, followed by Emily, Isabella, and Red. They entered a room that smelled of fresh-cut wood. Its walls were lined with books.

"Olive said a meal was waiting for us," said Isabella. "I don't see any food."

"Then we must go higher," said Red.

On the next floor of the treehouse, they found it—a beautiful oak table with legs carved into the shapes of forest animals. On the table were four plates, each loaded with five foods—roasted meat, an egg, mixed vegetables, lettuce, and a reddish paste. A silver cup was set beside each plate.

Aiden didn't like vegetables, and he wasn't sure about the reddish paste-like food, but he couldn't be choosy. Next to the table were slots where they could place their staffs. That way, the staffs stood upright and gave light in the darkness.

"Olive said we're supposed to eat in the midst of our enemies," said Isabella.

"Well, I'd say there are plenty of enemies outside this treehouse," noted Emily. "So...let's eat!"

"I was hoping for French fries, but this will have to do," said Red, climbing onto one of the chairs.

As they began to eat, the wind outside began to howl. Or was it the wolves? Then heavy rain lashed the side of the treehouse, followed by lightning and cracks of thunder.

Aiden closed the shutters of the two windows in the room. "Uh...you know, trees aren't a safe place to be during a lightning storm. Lightning strikes trees all the time."

"I think the Destroyers are trying to scare us out of the tree," said Emily, before taking a bite of her meat.

"You're probably right," said Aiden. "Our light protects us from many things. Let's pray that includes protecting us from lightning."

When Aiden took a bite of the reddish paste, he found that it was sweet—quite tasty. But he nearly choked on his food when a lightning blast struck right outside the treehouse. What's more, the storm wasn't the worst of it. They heard creatures scratching at the walls, trying to get in.

Suddenly, the shutters on the windows were thrown open violently, and two snarling Shadow Wolves began to climb in. As Aiden reached for his staff, he prayed that the darkness would not overcome the light.

TO BE CONTINUED ON PAGE 257.

DAY 34

JESUS SERVED TO FIX THIS BROKEN WORLD

DESTROYED!

Has someone ever destroyed or broken something very important or special to you? What happened? How did it make you feel? Draw the thing below or write about it.

THE BURNT BOOK

In the book *Little Women*, one of four sisters, Jo, loved writing. She spent years working on a book and considered it her pride and joy. But after a fight, Jo's youngest sister, Amy, burnt the special book in a fireplace. Read about what happened when Jo found out.

"My little book I was so fond of, and worked over, and meant to finish before Father got home? Have you really burned it?" said Jo, turning very pale, while her eyes kindled and her hands clutched Amy nervously.

"Yes, I did! I told you I'd make you pay for being so cross yesterday, and I have, so..."

Amy got no farther, for Jo's hot temper mastered her, and she shook Amy till her teeth chattered in her head, crying in a passion of grief and anger...

"You wicked, wicked girl! I never can write it again, and I'll never forgive you as long as I live."

Jo was furious about her book being destroyed because it was her creation—something she poured her love into. It's the same with God. He loves us so much that He gets angry when we hurt each other or ourselves.

In other words, getting mad about evil and loving something go together. That's why God can be angry and loving at the same time.

> **"The Lord is slow to anger and great in power, and the Lord will by no means clear the guilty. His way is in whirlwind and storm, and the clouds are the dust of his feet." Nahum 1:3 (ESV)**

MASTERPIECES ON DISPLAY

It is not easy for us to understand how God can be both angry and loving at the same time. But if He didn't get mad about sin, then that would mean our sin is not a big deal to Him. But it is a big deal! You are God's masterpiece just like the book was Jo's. But sin eats away at us, like fire consumes paper. God loves the world so much that He can't bear to see it destroyed.

Sin makes God very angry. In fact, God's anger at sin proves His love for us.

Besides, God doesn't lose His temper and fly off the handle. The Bible says He is **slow** to anger. It also says He is **great** in power. So, you do not want to mess with Him! He doesn't let the guilty off the hook. That is good news for us!

When something hurts or is unfair, it is not up to us to get revenge. God will take care of it.

> **"God claims Earth and everything in it, God claims World and all who live on it." Psalm 24:1 (MSG)**

God keeps things from falling apart. One way He does this is by holding back evil. In fact, a name for the Holy Spirit is the Great Restrainer.

One example of a restraint is handcuffs, so picture this: God put Satan in handcuffs! The Devil can't get you. Every day, God keeps evil from coming at you.

HOPE IN A TREE

Even though Satan is in handcuffs, sin still happens. We're still tempted, and when we keep giving in to sin, it slowly begins to destroy us. It changes us and breaks us down. This makes God angry because He loves us and hates to see us harmed—even when we're the ones hurting ourselves.

We had to be saved, not just from ourselves, but from God's anger. So, Jesus came to serve by taking all that anger on Himself. He served us to fix the world of its brokenness. He served us to give us hope.

> **"For there is hope for a tree, if it is cut down, that it will sprout again, and that its tender shoots will not cease." Job 14:7 (NKJV)**

Jesus was the tree that was cut down. But He came to life again. He brought us forgiveness of sins so that we too can forgive others in the same way.

Even though Jo said she would never forgive her sister, she eventually did forgive Amy for destroying the book. It was not easy, but Jo realized that having a sister was more important than her book.

Those Little Women had Big Hearts.

(For more on forgiveness, check out *Forgiving Challenge Kids* available at WWW.REDLETTERCHALLENGE.COM.)

CHALLENGE—RIGHTING A WRONG

Think about something unfair going on in the world right now. It could be hunger, a terrible accident, or bullying. Then, serve in a way that helps correct an unfairness in this world.

DAY 35

JESUS SERVED TO TAKE AWAY IMMEDIATE SUFFERING

THE GROCERY RUN

Kayla and her mom were grocery shopping when she noticed that her mom was buying double of everything. Her mom threw in two cans of green beans, two boxes of the same cereal, and two packets of stuffing mix.

"Mom, why are you buying two of each?" Kayla asked. "We're not going to eat all these things!"

"We're giving the extras away to the food pantry," her mom explained. "Many people in our city cannot afford groceries."

"Shouldn't we be telling these people about Jesus? Isn't that more important than a can of beans?" Kayla asked. "The kids probably don't even like beans," she added under her breath.

Kayla's mom thought long and hard about the question.

"Kayla, it's always important to tell people about Jesus. But sometimes we can also use our actions to share God's love, not just our words. Jesus healed people's suffering. He cares about those who are poor. The Bible says that if we have things and don't share, then God's love isn't in us."

Kayla saw another BOGO deal on pasta and ran to grab two boxes. She was glad she came along on this shopping trip. Although it meant double the groceries to carry, she was happy to help others in need. Sharing God's love with others was worth it!

OPEN YOUR HEART

Sometimes it's easy to think that God cares only about spiritual things like heaven, angels, and our souls. But from the very beginning, God has cared about the world and everyone and everything in it. That's why He called the world "good" after speaking the stars, earth, and animals into being. (He said "very good" after creating people.)

Taking care of the Earth is so important to God that He gave Adam the job of naming the animals and caring for the Garden of Eden. God also wants us to take care of His creation. He wants everyone to have clean water to drink, a safe place to live, and clothes to keep us warm. He hates sickness, war, and weather disasters. Those were never part of His plan. So, Jesus doesn't just care about people's hearts. He cares about their bodies too.

> **"But if anyone has the world's goods and sees his brother in need, yet closes his heart against him, how does God's love abide in him?"**
> **1 John 3:17 (ESV)**

These are serious words. If you don't love the poor, then you don't love God. But if you have faith, love will be there. If you are a Christian, you will serve others.

Service to others is a work of faith. If your faith is not accompanied by action, it is dead. The famous writer C.S. Lewis once compared faith and actions to a pair of scissors. The blades of a scissors are both important. If you didn't have both blades, how would a scissors even work? Faith and actions are like those two blades, working together.

When you have faith and understand you are saved by grace, you will be heartbroken for the poor. All "things" belong to God; they're not yours. So, God expects us to share the things He has given us—just like your parents teach you to share with your brothers, sisters, and friends.

Also, "poor" doesn't just mean not having money. The word "poor" in the Bible can refer to people who are old, mentally handicapped, depressed, refugees, immigrants, natural disaster victims, the unemployed, single parents, widows, or orphans. All these people are called "poor" in the Bible.

"Blessed are the poor in spirit, for theirs is the kingdom of heaven," Jesus said in Matthew 5:3 (NIV).

We are to love people as if they are Jesus. And one way to love them is to take care of their needs. Many organizations in our country and around the world serve the poor. Here are some examples:

- Habitat for Humanity helps people who cannot afford to build, fix, or improve their homes.

- Water Mission wants everyone to have clean, safe water to drink.

- Compassion International builds relationships so children can be helped out of poverty.

- The Red Cross protects and prevents human suffering worldwide through medical care.

- Samaritan's Purse helps people who are victims of war, natural disasters, famine, poverty, or persecution.

- Anthem of Hope helps people struggling with mental health.

- World Vision International provides food to children and families, helps people get clean water, and gives medicine to keep children healthy.

Service is not only spiritual. When we give someone a drink of water, buy extra groceries, or lend a helping hand, we share Jesus with them. We double our giving.

CHALLENGE—GET INVOLVED

Many different organizations help people. Choose one to get involved with today. You may want to get involved in one of the organizations listed earlier or talk to your pastor about ways you can help in your community through your church.

RED ALERT!

The Bible says Jesus died at the ninth hour, which is 3 p.m. Every day in the Temple, a spotless lamb was sacrificed at 3 p.m. In other words, Jesus, the spotless Savior, died on the cross at the same moment as a spotless lamb was sacrificed in the Temple.

DAY 36

JESUS SERVED TO SHOW US HOW IT'S DONE

LIVING LIKE THE POOR

One of the most famous servants in modern history was Mother Teresa, a Catholic nun and missionary to India. Her love for the poor, hungry, and homeless changed thousands of lives. She opened an orphanage, a leper colony, health clinics, and a nursing home.

In 1979, Mother Teresa won the Nobel Peace Prize and received $100,000 in prize money. She donated every bit of it to the poor. But Mother Teresa did not just help the poor. She lived like the poor. Here are some of the ways she did that:

- She ate only rice and salt.
- She had only three changes of clothes, which were made of rough cloth or old coats.
- She would patch her clothes instead of buying new ones.
- She had only one pair of shoes.
- To bathe, she used only a bucket of water.
- Even though it is swelteringly hot in India, she would not use a fan.

- She didn't own any radios or ways to play music.
- When she traveled, she would walk or take crowded buses.
- She slept on a hard mattress as poor people did.
- She cooked, washed, and even cleaned toilets, although there were other people on hand to do that.

Some said she was wasting her life and talents doing these "lowly" jobs. But Mother Teresa responded, "To some we are wasting our precious life and burying our talents…Our lives have no meaning unless we look at Christ and his poverty. Our work for the poor is a privilege and a gift to us."

Mother Teresa's work was the fruit of her life. God says that as children of God, we create fruit too.

GOOD ROOTS, GOOD FRUITS

If you've ever enjoyed a juicy orange or watermelon on a summer day or apples in the Fall, you know how tasty fruit can be. However, fruit is the part of the plant containing the seeds. So, it doesn't just taste good. It's vital for spreading seeds and growing more fruit.

That sounds just like our good actions. When we serve others, we spread the seeds of God's love, which grows and flourishes. Jesus put it this way:

> "For no good tree bears bad fruit, nor again does a bad tree bear good fruit, for each tree is known by its own fruit. For figs are not gathered from thorn bushes, nor are grapes picked from a bramble bush. The good person out of the good treasure of his heart produces good, and the evil person out of his evil treasure produces evil, for out of the abundance of the heart, his mouth speaks." **Luke 6:43-45 (ESV)**

In other words, Jesus says good trees give us good fruit, while bad trees give us bad fruit. So, how do we become a tree that produces good fruit?

To produce good fruits, we need good roots.

Jesus is our root. When we are rooted in the teachings and person of Jesus, we can't help but produce good fruit.

Any good things we do come from Jesus, the root of our life. Left on our own, we will wither and die. As Mother Teresa said, "Be kind and merciful. Let no one ever come to you without coming away better and happier."

Her words sound a lot like what the Apostle Paul said. **"Be kind and compassionate to one another, forgiving each other, just as in Christ God forgave you." Ephesians 4:32 (NIV)**

Live like Jesus. He doesn't sit up in heaven, pouring down blessings whenever we need them. Instead, Jesus showed the truest love by coming down into our mess. He was born as a baby. He grew up, went to school, got hurt, and had sleepless nights. He knew what it meant to be hungry, lonely, and tired. It wasn't easy, but Jesus lived with people as He loved them.

But Jesus is not just a good example. He is our Savior. We can never take His place, but we can follow in His footsteps. Jesus still serves you today. And when you follow Jesus, as Mother Teresa did, you will see the fruit of your love.

And that's the tastiest fruit of all.

CHALLENGE—FIND CREATIVE WAYS TO GIVE

The next time you shop, pick the less expensive item. Use the extra money you saved to buy something for someone else. As that habit grows, you will have more and more you can give.

RED ALERT!

God saved us with "gopher wood." That's the wood that Noah used to build the ark, although no one knows what tree produced gopher wood. Whatever it was, God saved Noah and his family thanks to that tree.

DAY 37

JESUS SERVED TO SAVE US FROM OUR DEATH SENTENCE

DOUBTING JOHN

Imagine you were falsely accused of a crime and had to go to jail. What would you bring with you if you could pack just one small bag? Draw or write out your packing list below.

John the Baptist was put in jail just for preaching about Jesus (and getting Herod Antipas angry). Talk about an unfair arrest! John spent his life telling people that Jesus had come. He had been so sure of what he was supposed to do, but now, as he sat in a dark jail, he began to have doubts. You may have heard of Doubting Thomas. But we don't often talk about Doubting John.

"Maybe it was all a big mistake," John thought as he stewed in jail. "I'll send a message to Jesus, to see if He is really the One we have been waiting for because I am starting to wonder."

When Jesus saw the message, He wanted to calm John's fears. This is what Jesus said:

> "...the blind see, the lame walk, those with leprosy are cured, the deaf hear, the dead are raised to life, and the Good News is being preached to the poor." Matthew 11:5 (NLT)

Jesus comforted John the Baptist by reminding him of the miracles He did. From that point on, John knew Jesus was truly the Son of God.

EVERY EMOTION

Jesus cares about our hurts because He experienced ALL the emotions that people feel! We are trained to think we should be happy all the time. But caring or being sad for another person is just as important. That's why our caring connection is found in our vagus nerve (talked about on Day 23) right next to our body's control of breathing and eating. That's not an accident! Caring is as natural as breathing.

Read the following verses. Then color in the symbols for the emotions you see in Jesus in these verses. (Some verses may have more than one emotion.)

1 JESUS AND THE FIG TREE

"As they left Bethany the next day, he [Jesus] was hungry. Off in the distance he saw a fig tree in full leaf. He came up to it expecting to find something for breakfast, but found nothing but fig leaves. (It wasn't yet the season for figs.) He addressed the tree: 'No one is going to eat fruit from you again—ever!'" Mark 11:12-14a (MSG)

Emotions Jesus Felt:

Angry   Hungry   Thirsty   Frustrated   Alone   Sad

2 JESUS IN THE TEMPLE

"Jesus went straight to the Temple and threw out everyone who had set up shop, buying and selling. He kicked over the tables of loan sharks and the stalls of dove merchants. He quoted this text: 'My house was designated a house of prayer; You have made it a hangout for thieves.'" Matthew 21:12-13 (MSG)

Emotions Jesus Felt:

Angry   Hungry   Thirsty   Frustrated   Alone   Sad

"Then Jesus went with them to a garden called Gethsemane and told his disciples, 'Stay here while I go over there and pray.' Taking along Peter and the two sons of Zebedee, he plunged into an agonizing sorrow. Then he said, 'This sorrow is crushing my life out. Stay here and keep vigil with me.'

"Going a little ahead, he fell on his face, praying, 'My Father, if there is any way, get me out of this. But please, not what I want. You, what do *you* want?'

"When he came back to his disciples, he found them sound asleep. He said to Peter, 'Can't you stick it out with me a single hour? Stay alert; be in prayer so you don't wander into temptation without even knowing you're in danger. There is a part of you that is eager, ready for anything in God. But there's another part that's as lazy as an old dog sleeping by the fire.'" Matthew 26:36-41 (MSG)

Emotions Jesus Felt:

Angry   Hungry   Thirsty   Frustrated   Alone   Sad

THE FOREVER HEALING

Jesus healed people in the Bible because He felt sorry for them. But those physical healings didn't last forever because none of those people are still alive today. So, does that mean God's power didn't last?

No, God's healing power did what it was supposed to do. It healed the sickness. But they were still stuck in their jail of sin.

So, Jesus went straight to the heart of the matter. He wanted to give people a healing that would last forever. He gave them forgiveness.

The people who were physically healed grew old and eventually died. But those whom Jesus forgave are still forgiven. Jesus's forgiveness lasts forever.

There are many sick people in the world right now. You might even know one. Some people do not understand why everyone isn't healed by Jesus. They think it is unfair or mean of God to not heal every sick person. They do not understand that Jesus wants to give us something that is bigger and better than getting a healed body for a short time. Jesus wants to give us a Forever Life.

In heaven, everyone will have a new body that will never die. Moreover, that new body will be perfect. When we put our trust in Jesus, the Bible describes us as a tree planted next to a stream.

> **"He is like a tree planted by water, that sends out its roots by the stream, and does not fear when heat comes, for its leaves remain green, and is not anxious in the year of drought, for it does not cease to bear fruit."**
> **Jeremiah 17:8 (ESV)**

FOREVER FREEDOM

Jesus is our "get out of jail free" card. He has declared us free from the prison of our sin. We no longer face a death sentence, but we have a new life in Jesus! Imagine what it would be like to be thrown into a deep, dark dungeon, where there is no light. Then, one day, the doors are thrown open and you are told to walk free forever.

That's what Jesus did for us.

Jesus doesn't heal everyone's "right now" hurts, but He died so everyone could be given a "right relationship forever" life. And that is the greatest miracle of all!

CHALLENGE—PRISON PRAYERS

Pray for those in prison. If God is calling you to do more, donate money to local organizations that help those in jail. You could also send a message of encouragement or team up with organizations that support those coming out of jail or prison and help them adjust to their new life.

RED ALERT!

In the Old Testament, Israel was sometimes symbolized by a fig tree. So, when Jesus cursed the fig tree for not producing fruit, it was His way of criticizing Israel for not being fruitful—for not giving their hearts to God.

DAY 38

JESUS SERVED TO INCLUDE US IN HIS MINISTRY

THE LARGEST TREE IN THE WORLD

In the capital of West Bengal in India, tourists flock to a forest where you can walk amid over 3,000 trees covering more than three and a half acres. But this is no ordinary forest. In fact, it isn't a forest at all. It is **one** giant tree called the Great Banyan Tree. This unique tree is 250 years old and keeps growing every year. In 1989, the tree was officially listed in *The Guinness Book of World Records* for being the largest tree in the world.

The tree trunks you see in this "forest" are actually roots called "aerial roots." These are roots that grow aboveground in the air. Get it? AIR-ial! Each individual aerial root looks like a separate tree, standing on its own, but it is connected to all the other roots underground. Each root does not live for itself. They work together!

People are more like the aerial roots of a single tree than a forest of individual trees. We may look like a single human, but deep down, we are connected to something bigger that others cannot see. Also, like the Banyan tree, our work is not just for us. We help a bigger body. We are all part of one living thing—the Body of Christ.

In the space below, draw the underground roots that connect these aboveground aerial roots to each other.

WE'RE INCLUDED IN GOD'S WORK

God's plan, from the very beginning, was to include us in His work. In the Garden of Eden, Adam and Eve were given the job to rule over every living creature.

"God spoke: 'Let us make human beings in our image, make them reflecting our nature so they can be responsible for the fish in the sea,

the birds in the air, the cattle, and, yes, Earth itself, and every animal that moves on the face of Earth.'" Genesis 1:26 (MSG)

Adam and Eve served in the garden by taking care of every animal. They were part of God's plan. Serving wasn't a punishment. It was a privilege! However, the animals were not their property to do whatever they wanted with. Their job was to give them the best life possible.

Today, we're no longer in the Garden of Eden, but God still invites us to be a part of His work. Imagine if the President of the United States called and asked you to work on something for the country. It's even more amazing that God is calling you. He's asking you to work for Him!

Serving is a team thing.

THE NEEDS OF OTHERS

Serving means we "give up on piling up." It means you don't pile up possessions for yourself alone. You don't work to meet your needs only. Serving means caring about the needs of others as well. In other words…

Serving is an "others" thing.

As it says in Acts 20:35 (ESV), **"In all things I have shown you that by working hard in this way we must help the weak and remember the words of the Lord Jesus, how he himself said, 'It is more blessed to give than to receive.'"**

Because of sin, serving can feel challenging because we are selfish. Giving up what we want is difficult. But even though it is hard, God says serving is the best thing for us. Here is what happens when you serve:

- You will think less about your own problems.
- You won't feel lonely.
- You will feel part of a greater cause.
- It feels good to help others.
- You will be more thankful when you see the problems others have to face.

So, you see…by focusing on the needs of others, you improve your life in the process!

Serving is not always easy, but it is always worth it. After all, it was worth it to Jesus.

> **"We do this by keeping our eyes on Jesus, the champion who initiates and perfects our faith. Because of the joy awaiting him, he [Jesus] endured the cross, disregarding its shame. Now he is seated in the place of honor beside God's throne." Hebrews 12:2 (NLT)**

The joy that awaited Jesus made all His suffering worth it. That joy is YOU! For Jesus, you were worth the suffering. Jesus served so that we could be included in God's work. This isn't a "HAVE to" thing… it's a "GET to" thing!

CHALLENGE—CHURCH SERVANTS

Serve with your church. You are part of something bigger, and when you join forces with others, you can help in a big way.

DAY 39

JESUS SERVED TO
SHOW US HEAVEN

WATER PARK

One hot summer day, Kara and her three-year-old brother, Drew, went to the waterpark. Her mom parked the car and loaded the stroller with swimsuits, sunscreen, snacks, and floaties. Then they got in line to buy tickets.

Drew found it all boring. At three years old, he had no idea what a water park even was. Suddenly, a sprinkler shot from the ground to water the grass along the sidewalk.

"Why don't you take Drew to the sprinkler while I wait in line?" Kara's mom suggested.

Drew loved the sprinkler! He stood next to it and giggled as the water tickled his stomach and legs. He covered the sprinkler with his hand and watched in fascination as the water squirted between his fingers. Then he stomped in the muddy puddle beneath the sprinkler. The cool water soaked his sandals. This was awesome!

Suddenly, Drew felt a tug on his arm.

"Come on, Drew! Time to go!" Kara said excitedly. But Drew did not want to leave. He had been sitting in his car seat and stroller for hours and wanted to stay by the sprinkler. His mother came over and tried to coax him. "Come on, Drewie, we're going to play in the water!"

But Drew had water right here. As his mother picked him up to return him to his stroller, he began howling at the top of his lungs.

"Spinker! Spinker!" he cried, tears rolling down his cheeks. Even though fun lay ahead at the water park, Drew was leaving the best thing he had seen that day, and he was mad.

It's easy to smile at a toddler who doesn't understand what amazing things are ahead of him at a water park, but sometimes we too can act like Drew. We become so excited about what is in front of us that we forget all the amazing things God has in store for us, both here on Earth and in heaven someday.

Like Drew with the waterpark, we do not know what heaven is like because we've never been there. It's hard to be excited about a place we don't understand. This is one of the reasons Jesus came to serve. When Jesus serves, He gives us a glimpse of what heaven is like. The more we are served by God, the better we understand heaven.

DANIEL'S VISIONS

The prophet Daniel is famous for the story of the Lion's Den, but did you know that the book of Daniel also has visions and dreams about heaven? Read about one of his visions below.

"The visions of my head as I lay in bed were these: I saw, and behold, a tree in the midst of the earth, and its height was great. The tree grew and became strong, and its top reached to heaven, and it was visible to the end of the whole earth. Its leaves were beautiful and its fruit abundant, and in it was food for all. The beasts of the field found shade under it, and the birds of the heavens lived in its branches, and all flesh was fed from it. Daniel 4:10-12 (ESV)

Daniel saw a great tree growing on the earth—a tree so big and wonderful that it took care of every person and animal in the world. Unfortunately, I don't think Daniel meant that heaven would be a giant treehouse (although that sure would be fun).

The tree was Jesus.

Jesus is big enough for everyone to see Him. He is the only one who could reach heaven from Earth. God provides the whole Earth with food, air, water, and sunshine. He also is the shelter we need.

The tree in Daniel's vision was a strong, sturdy servant, protecting and feeding all of Earth's creatures. And as if that wasn't enough, it was beautiful, and its branches were as high as heaven. What a wonderful glimpse of paradise.

So, whether we think of heaven as an endless waterpark or a magnificent tree, it's going to be glorious. But until we get there, let's serve each other. Although serving may not always seem like fun, there is more fun in store for you in heaven than you can even imagine.

Get ready to splash in the goodness of God and climb trees to your heart's delight!

CHALLENGE—TRADING SCREENS FOR SERVING

Give up fifteen minutes of your normal screen time to serve someone else today. While it may be hard to turn off your device early, trust that what God has in store for you is way better than some show you won't even remember tomorrow.

RED ALERT!

Jewish people today celebrate Passover with a Seder meal. During this meal, three pieces of unleavened bread (matzah) are set aside. The middle piece is broken in half, and the larger half is wrapped in linen and hidden for children to find later. Jewish Christians believe that this bread, wrapped in linen and hidden, is a symbol of Christ's body, which was wrapped in cloth and hidden in a tomb.

DAY 40

JESUS SERVED TO GIVE US EVERYTHING

THE GIVING TREE

In the book *The Giving Tree*, by Shel Silverstein, a tree gives parts of herself away to a boy as he grows. She gives him her branches, leaves, apples, and trunk until there is just a stump left. In the end, when the boy is an old man, the stump becomes a chair for him to sit on.

The author once said the story was about one person who takes and another person who gives. However, the serving done by the tree is different from the kind of serving that Jesus did.

Here are some differences between how Jesus serves us and how the tree served the boy.

The Giving Tree	**Jesus**
The boy must come to the tree.	Jesus came to us.
The boy must ask for things from the tree.	Jesus knows what we need before we even ask.
The tree's gifts don't last.	Jesus's gifts last forever.
The tree cannot help the boy with all his problems.	Jesus can be there for every one of our problems.
The tree did not give everything. It still had its stump and roots.	Jesus gave everything by dying. Because He gave everything, He gained everything. He offers us everything, too.

If you tried to give like the Giving Tree, you would eventually run out of what you can do for others. You would become a stump, not able to do much.

But God's giving is endless. He is like a well filled with an endless supply of water. We'll never run out of His love.

Jesus did not have to die for us, but He did it anyway. And the moment He rose from the dead, He changed everything for you—and the world. His gift of eternal life is all you need. God gives us above and beyond what we need—gifts from above.

Think about your own life as you read the following poem. What gifts have God given you?

The Giving God

Once there was a God who loved you.
His love for you was strong and true.
God saved you from some nasty sin
And sticks with you through thick
    and thin.
All that would have been enough.

God made a world where you
    can grow.
He gave you trees and stars aglow.
You have a bed and place called home
And clothes to wear and shoes
    to roam.
All that would have been enough.

God wanted you to feel secure,
So He gave you gifts that will endure.
He gave you water and food to eat.
And legs and arms and eyes and feet.
All that would have been enough.

It was important to God that you
    belong.
So He gave you a family, connected
    and strong,
He gave you friends to help you
    dream,
A church and pals who are on your
    team.
All that would have been enough.

You are one of a kind. There are
    no copies!
God gave you strengths and many
    hobbies.
He made some to sing and some
    to build,
And all with gifts so we'd be fulfilled.
All that would have been enough.

And still, God wants you to try your
    best.
Give your all and trust God with the
    rest.
God has ideas and plans that come
    from above,
And while watching you live, His heart
    bursts with love.
All that would have been enough.

Since God made you, He knows your
    heart.
He cares 'cause you're His work of art.
He calls you to love as He has loved
    you.
Serving is loving. It's holy and true.
And that is more than enough.

Note: The final line, "that would have been enough," is based on the Hebrew word *dayenu*, which means just that. It comes from the traditional Passover song of the same name.

THE GO-BETWEEN TREE

If God is in heaven in the sky, and if He created the first human (Adam) of dirt, which is part of the ground, then we need something to join heaven and earth. What can touch the dirt down below and also stretch high into the sky?

A tree.

The cross was cut from what?

A tree.

The cross is our reminder that we need a connection to God.

One name for Jesus is "mediator." That means He is the in-between person for us and God.

Because of Jesus, we are forgiven. God isn't stuck far away in the sky, out of reach. He came down to earth and now lives in each of our hearts. He is with us everywhere we go. The Holy Spirit is always with us.

Because of the cross, we can be with God. You might even say that Jesus's cross is like a ladder connecting us with God. And through His cross, Jesus serves us as we serve others.

THE CROSS IS THE TREE OF LIFE. It is the true Giving Tree.

"Therefore, as you received Christ Jesus the Lord, so walk in him, rooted and built up in him and established in the faith, just as you were taught, abounding in thanksgiving." Colossians 2:6-7 (ESV)

CHALLENGE—THE GO-BETWEEN TREE

Draw a tree below, connecting the sky with earth. Then draw a cross next to it.

You are connected to God because of Jesus. Any serving you do is only because you have been served by Him. Now plant a real tree or flower. When you plant a tree, you are helping God's creation become more like heaven, just as He wants it.

RED ALERT!

When Adam and Eve disobeyed God in the Garden of Eden, they broke a "covenant" with God—an agreement or promise. God had every right to destroy them, but He chose a different way—redemption. He decided to save them by punishing His Son, Jesus, in our place.

#SERVINGCHALLENGEKIDS

WHAT NOW?

TREE-MENDOUS!

Congratulations! You finished our 40-day hike through the Serving Challenge. But before we say farewell, let's touch on a few more things—beginning with your thumbs. Yes, your thumbs.

Use an inkpad or a washable marker to color your thumb. Then put your thumbprint in the box below. What similarities do you see between your fingerprint and the annual rings of a tree?

Your fingerprint is your very own. No two fingerprints are alike. Even identical twins have their own sets of fingerprints. That's why police use fingerprints to figure out who was at the scene of a crime.

Fingerprints are formed when you are only three inches long in your mother's womb. Layers of skin grow so quickly that they swirl and buckle around each other, causing the little ridges to stand up in unique formations.

Fingerprints are divided into three kinds:

THE ARCH   THE WHORL   THE LOOP

The arch is the rarest. Only 5 percent of the population has it. Roughly 25 to 35 percent of people have a whorl fingerprint, while the loop is the most popular, found in 60 to 70 percent of the population.

Look at the thumbprint you made. Which kind of fingerprint do you have?

Your fingerprints are not the only special and unique thing about you. God says we are all fearfully and wonderfully made. (Psalm 139:14) Every part of you is wonderful and made for a purpose. You are not supposed to be like everyone else. Our unique talents are given to us as gifts, and we should do our best with them.

WINNING ISN'T EVERYTHING

Sometimes it's easy to confuse **doing** your best and **being** the best. Every person in the world wants to hear "good job" or "well done." It feels good to get first place in something, and people give you a lot of attention when you win. It is tempting to want to be perfect all the time at what you do.

It's not a bad thing to want your mom and dad to be proud of you, your teachers to notice you, and your friends to like you. But when that becomes the most important thing, you will hate to fail. You will quit if you don't win all the time. Winning and being first can become the most important thing in the world. But they're not.

What words do you want to hear the most? Fill in the blank below.

Well done, good and faithful _____.

In Matthew 25:23 (NIV), Jesus does NOT say, "Well done, good and faithful athlete..."

Or... ~~Dancer~~   ~~Gamer~~   ~~Actor~~

~~A+ Student~~   ~~YouTuber~~   ~~Singer~~

~~Popular Friend to Everyone~~

Jesus says...

"Well done, good and faithful...servant."

Nothing else will heal your heart except hearing God say this to you. But hold on...we aren't always faithful and good, right? So how can we be sure that God will say this to us? What about those times that we don't do our best? Or when winning is the most important thing to us?

Because of Jesus, God can still call you "good." His forgiveness covers all those times when you aren't faithful or good. Forgiveness is free. It's not something we work to earn. You don't serve as a way to trick God into liking you or to win brownie points with Him. You are not trying to earn God's love. You do servant acts because you are thankful, and you love Jesus.

God can call you faithful because Jesus was faithful.

Many famous people have served in amazing ways. You learned about some of them, such as Mother Teresa, Louis Braille, and Felipe Merioles. But how is Jesus different?

First, these other servants are all human. They never claimed to be God, but Jesus is Lord. Second, Jesus served us perfectly. The other servants were flawed, like all humans.

Jesus Christ came into the world and said, "My life is to serve you. My life is poured out for you. I sacrificed for you." Jesus Christ is the King of Kings, but He's also the Servant of Servants. He's our Servant King, and He will take care of you, even when hard times come. He's our North Star, and He will lead you when you're lost.

Jesus is the Way, and that makes all the difference in the world.

HAVE FUN COLORING THIS PAGE!
FIND MORE LIKE THIS AT SERVINGCHALLENGE.COM/FREE-KIDS-RESOURCES

THE FOREST OF REDVALE

PART 7

Two Shadow Wolves leaped through the treehouse windows and landed on the floor, skidding on the wood.

Isabella screamed as she leaped from her chair. She grabbed her staff, with the light burning on its tip, and jabbed it at the wolves. A third Shadow Wolf, its body as dark as tar, sprang through the window but immediately came face to face with Aiden and Emily and their wooden staffs.

"The light shines in the darkness!" Emily shouted.

"And the darkness has not overcome it!" added Aiden.

The Perez kids used their staffs, blazing with light, to drive the three Shadow Wolves out of the treehouse and back into the darkness. Outside, in the Valley of Shadows, rain poured, lightning sizzled, and branches came crashing down as the storm raged.

When it appeared that the wolves were not coming back immediately, Red closed the shattered shutters and motioned toward the table. "We better hurry and finish this meal. For some reason, Olive wants us to eat this meal in the presence of our enemies."

"It doesn't make sense to me, but Olive's been right all along," said Isabella, rushing back to her seat at the table. As she did, she spied something in the corner of the room that wasn't there before.

It was a basin of water and a hand towel.

Isabella recalled how Jesus washed His disciples' feet at the Last Supper—the night before He died on the cross. Then she glanced down at her shoes, which were caked with mud from the hike into the valley. She made a beeline for the water basin.

"Come back here!" Aiden shouted. "We gotta finish this meal before the wolves return! That water is for washing up after we eat."

"I don't think so." Carrying the basin of water and setting it before her sister, Isabella crouched, reaching for Emily's right foot.

Emily yanked her foot back. "What're you doing?"

"I'm washing your feet."

"Huh?"

"Remember, we're Servanteers," Isabella said. "I think we're meant to wash each other's feet—like servants do. Like Jesus did."

"I'm not touching anyone's smelly feet!" Aiden burst.

"Look who's talking," said Isabella. "After you play basketball, I can smell your gym shoes from downstairs!"

As Isabella dipped the towel in the water, two Shadow Wolves returned, this time knocking the windows' shutters completely off their hinges. The monsters howled and growled and snapped—but Aiden jabbed his staff at them, keeping them from entering.

"Hurry, hurry, hurry, I think they're trying to stop what you're doing!" Aiden shouted.

Isabella dipped the cloth in the warm water and began to clean the dirt coating her sister's feet. She tried to ignore the fury of the wolves as she scrubbed Emily's right foot, then her left. While she did, she smelled the faint perfume of flowers rising from the water.

"Now my turn!" Emily removed Isabella's shoe and began to scrub. The smell of flowers grew stronger, and the wolves went even wilder.

When Emily finished, Isabella took up her staff and tapped Aiden on the shoulder. "I'll keep the wolves away. It's your turn to have your feet washed."

Aiden shook his head fiercely. "Nobody's washing my feet! That's weird!"

"C'mon, Aiden! I think it's part of our test!" Emily approached with the wet cloth, but Aiden dodged out of her way. He nearly ran right into the snapping jaws of one of the Shadow Wolves, which suddenly lunged through the window.

That close call must have scared him because he said, "Oh, all right! Just get it over with. Quickly!"

When Emily removed his first shoe, she gasped and gagged, and so did Isabella. Aiden's foot was as stinky as spoiled salmon. But as she scrubbed his feet, the scent of flowers filled the room—and the wolves finally began to retreat.

"See!" shouted Isabella. "When we wash each other's feet, the wolves become terrified!"

"All right, you made your point!" Aiden said.

"What about me?" asked Red. "I don't have shoes, so my feet are the muddiest of all."

"I will wash your feet," came a voice from below.

The voice rose from the spiral staircase, as heavy footsteps sounded on the stairs. Setting aside her wet towel, Emily snatched up her staff. She was ready for whatever creature was coming up the stairs.

"Stay back!" she shouted. "We've got the light on our side!"

"That's good," said the voice. "We should all have the light on our side." Then, in the greatest, most wonderful of surprises, Malachi's head popped through the trapdoor in the floor. He rose from below, climbing the final stair and stepping into the room.

FOG AND SHADOW

Emily dropped her staff and ran into his arms, spilling tears of joy.

"Malachi, you're alive!"

Red danced on the table.

They all hugged as one, arms entwined like the branches and roots of trees.

"But how?" asked Aiden. "How did you defeat so many wolves when you were attacked on the hill?"

"I didn't defeat them," said Malachi, motioning for Red and the kids to return to their seats. "I will tell you all that happened as you finish your meal in haste. You must dine in the presence of your enemies for the Great Change to begin."

As they dug into their food, Malachi washed Red's feet and spun his story.

"The Fog Wolves dragged me deep into the woods, where they planned to kill me. But as they argued about who would get to bite first, I asked them what their hearts most desired."

"And what did they say?" asked Emily before taking a bite of food.

"They answered me honestly. The Fog Wolves said their greatest desire was to be real wolves, not made of fog. As the Good Book says, we're 'nothing but a wisp of fog, catching a brief bit of sun before disappearing.' They wanted to be solid—more than wisps of fog."

"And you did that for them?"

"No, the King did it for them—at least he offered it to all of them," Malachi said, rising to take a seat. "The wolves that didn't reject the King's gift now roam the forest, and they're as real as this table." Malachi knocked on the wood.

"You mean some didn't choose to be real?" Isabella asked. "But when they saw the other wolves become solid, become real, I would have thought all of them would happily accept the gift from the King."

"Unfortunately, some rejected it. They didn't like the idea of serving anyone. They wanted to be kings of their own life. So, they chose to remain lords of the fog, a kingdom of the air. Their kingdom is fleeting, here today and gone tomorrow."

"How sad," said Emily.

"The Fog Wolves that became real saved you today. They drove away the Shadow Wolves attacking the treehouse. So, you have them to thank."

"I was wondering why it got so quiet out there all of a sudden," said Aiden.

"But if the Fog Wolves could serve the King and become real, maybe the same thing can happen to the Shadow Wolves," said Isabella.

"There is hope for everyone, including Shadow Wolves. They, too, desire to be real. As the Good Book says…"

"'Mortals, born of woman, are of few days and full of trouble. They spring up like flowers and wither away; like fleeting shadows, they do not endure,'" said Isabella, finishing his sentence. "That's Job 14, verses one and two."

"So, let's go to the Shadow Wolves!" said Aiden, grabbing his staff. "We must tell them they can become real!"

"In due time," said Malachi. "Now that you have completed your meal, we first need to see how Olive and Jesse are doing."

Emily's heart nearly stopped. In all the excitement, she had completely forgotten about their two new friends.

Leaping to her feet, Emily scrambled down the spiral staircase, without even bothering to put her shoes back on. She figured her brother or sister could just wash her feet again.

When Emily hit the ground, she found Olive and Jesse standing about fifteen feet from the treehouse. And the first thing she spotted was an enormous crack in Olive's bark. It was a large wound—much larger than the crack that the Humongous Fungus had put into the side of a tree.

With tears in her eyes, Emily put her hand on the olive tree's bark. "Oh Olive, I'm so sorry! Does it hurt badly?"

"It does, little one, it does."

Then, with her heart breaking, Emily wrapped her arms around Olive's trunk—although her arms couldn't go all the way around. "I'm so sorry, Olive. Is there anything I can do to help?"

"You're helping right now, little one."

"I only wish my arms could wrap around you completely," she said.

"They can—with our help," said Isabella, who also hugged the trunk, linking hands with Emily.

"Don't mind if I do," added Aiden, and he too hugged Olive, linking hands with Isabella. Then Red and Malachi joined. With all five connected as one, their arms wrapped all the way around Olive's trunk.

As they completed the chain of hands around the tree, Emily felt a sudden, soothing warmth spread across her entire body, and a golden glow broke out from the wound in Olive's bark. Emily squeezed even tighter, holding on to Olive for dear life. The golden light shot up through Olive's trunk, spreading out among all her branches. It became so bright that Emily had to close her eyes.

She never wanted to let go. But, eventually, she felt Malachi's gentle hands on her shoulder, drawing her away. And when she stepped back, she beheld a wonder.

Olive had become a Tree of Light, golden and alive.

THE SHEPHERD KING

Through it all, Aiden didn't forget Jesse. When he turned to the tree stump, he found that Jesse had also been filled, inside and out, with the golden light. The plant growing from his head burst into a beautiful crown of flowers.

"This is the greatest day of my life!" Jesse, the grumbler, began to hop around and dance. He couldn't stop laughing.

Meanwhile, the light also spread across the ground, lighting up the soil with a brilliant golden glow. The glow flowed through the roots of all the trees in the forest, like rivers of gold branching out in all directions.

The skeleton trees came to life. Leaves sprouted on their branches—and then flowers of all colors burst into view, like fireworks. Many of the branches also sprouted fruit—apples, oranges, pears…and even olives.

Malachi beamed. "As the Good Book says, 'Then the angel showed me the river of the water of life, as clear as crystal, flowing from the throne of God and of the Lamb down the middle of the great street of the city. On each side of the river stood the tree of life, bearing twelve crops of fruit, yielding its fruit every month. And the leaves of the tree are for the healing of the nations.'"

But the surprises were not over yet. Aiden heard the bleating of sheep and saw a shepherd with his small flock emerge from the forest. As the shepherd came closer, with a staff in his hand, Aiden recognized his face. It was the King of Redvale, but he wasn't wearing his royal robes. He was dressed as a simple shepherd.

Suddenly, three Shadow Wolves darted from the left. They sprinted toward one of the smaller sheep, separated from the rest of the flock. Aiden was sure the wolves were going to kill the lamb.

But the three wolves stopped short. They began to whimper, like dogs, and they bowed their heads before the Shepherd King. The King crouched to their level, put his hand on each of their backs, and petted them. As he did, they slowly changed from shadows to real wolves. Then they bounded into the forest, bursting with new life.

The Shepherd King rose and strode forward, staff in hand.

"Well done, good and faithful servants!" he declared, his voice echoing across the valley.

One of the smaller trees in the forest scurried up to the Shepherd King, bowed, and handed him three wreaths.

"Aiden, step forward," the King announced.

Aiden knelt on one knee as the Shepherd King placed a wreath on his head.

"Well done, good and faithful Aiden," said the King. "You served, even when it hurt. Your arms ached when you held up the staff, but you did it anyway because you wanted to save the trees from the beetles. Thank you for your strong arms."

Next was Isabella. The Shepherd King placed a wreath on her head. "Well done, good and faithful Isabella. You served, even when you were afraid. You brought Living Water to heal the wounds of a dying tree. Thank you for your strong heart."

Finally, the Shepherd King turned his eyes on Emily. She bowed her head. The Shepherd King put a hand beneath her chin and raised her face to meet his eyes. "Well done, good and faithful Emily. You served, even when you expected no praise."

"But that's not true," said Emily, lowering her head once more. "When I tried to help the beetle, I did it for praise."

Again, the Shepherd King lifted her head. "That was true then. But when you hugged Olive, you expected no praise. You did it from love. Pure love, as pure as Living Water, healed Olive. Well done, good and faithful servant."

Emily glowed from the inside when the Shepherd King placed the wreath on her head.

HOMEWARD BOUND

Sadly, Isabella knew what was coming next.

The Shepherd King motioned toward the treehouse. "It is time."

It was time to go home. They had accomplished their mission.

"The staffs are yours to keep," said the King. "A shepherd's staff is meant to fend off wolves and guide sheep to safety. Use them wisely."

"Thank you," said Isabella. She had been hoping they could keep their staffs, and she wondered if they would have any power back at home.

After sharing sad farewells all around, Isabella, Emily, and Aiden climbed the spiral staircase, entering the first floor of the treehouse. Then they climbed to the second floor. Then the third floor. And the fourth. And the fifth. And the sixth.

"I don't remember the treehouse being this big," Aiden said when they reached the seventh floor.

"It's bigger on the inside," noted Isabella.

Next: An eighth, ninth, tenth, and eleventh floors.

"I'm not sure it's ever going to end," came a voice from behind.

Isabella glanced back and saw Red right behind them. "Red, what are you doing?"

"I don't want to say goodbye. Do you mind if I walk with you to the end?"

"Of course, we don't mind," said Emily, giving Red a kiss on the nose.

Finally, on the twelfth floor, they ran out of staircases and faced a door with the carving of an enormous olive tree on it.

"I think this is where we say goodbye," said Aiden, lifting Red and squeezing him with a hug.

"Farewell, my friends!" called the fox. "I'll miss you!"

Isabella led the way, swinging open the door and stepping into the darkness. As she did, she heard Red shout, "Wait, you dropped something!"

Then Isabella stepped from the darkness and into her living room. She was home, soon followed by Aiden, Emily…

…and Red?

"Oops," said Red, looking shocked at finding himself in the Perez children's house. He held out Isabella's smart phone. "You dropped this."

"Thanks." Isabella took the phone and slid it back into her pocket. The phone probably worked again in their world, but Isabella didn't feel much like using it. After all the excitement and adventure, going back to the world of screens would seem rather dull.

Red wandered around their living room, then bounced on the couch. "Wow! Sooooo, this is where you live! Comfy!"

"Uh, Red, how are you going to get back to Redvale?" Isabella asked.

Red's smile vanished in an instant. "That's a very good question. I don't think Malachi meant for me to be here."

When they heard footsteps coming up from the basement, Red looked around for a hiding spot.

"Quick!" said Isabella. "Follow us! Our rooms are upstairs!"

Isabella had never seen the fox move so fast. When they reached Isabella's room, Red dove under the covers of her bed.

"What are we going to do?" Emily asked. "How are we going to explain him to Mom and Dad?"

"I could tell your parents I'm a new kid in school," said Red, peeking his head from under the covers.

Aiden laughed. "I think they're going to know you're not a new kid."

"Whatever you do, don't talk to people," said Emily. "Foxes in our world don't talk."

"That's a bummer," said Red. "Maybe I can teach them."

"We'll figure something out," said Isabella.

"In the meantime, would you like to do some planting?" Red said, holding out his paw and opening it. Nestled in his paw were three seeds. "These are olive tree seeds."

Isabella smiled. "Olive seeds from Redvale? Will they grow in our world?"

"There's one way to find out."

So, the three Perez children hurried out to their backyard, grabbed a shovel from the garage, and planted the three seeds. They marked the spots by driving their staffs into the ground. Red helped, but he had to dive into a clump of bushes when their parents came out to see what they were doing.

That night, Red and the kids stood at the window of Aiden's room, which looked down on the backyard. The three staffs, where the three seeds had been planted, shone in the glow of a nearby streetlight.

"We'll name the trees Olive, Jesse, and Red," Isabella said.

"Oooo, I like that," said Red.

Isabella glanced at the little fox, who sat on Emily's shoulders as he gazed out the window. "Oh, Red, you're a long way from home. How are we going to get you back?"

"We'll find a way," said Red. "Besides, when I'm with all of you, I am home."

Isabella put a hand on the fox's back and looked out the window. Would the three trees grow overnight, as they did in Redvale? They would soon find out when the morning star rose the next day.

They were new creations, Isabella pondered. The old had passed away. Behold, the new had come.

– THE END –

SOURCES

Alcott, Louisa M. (2004). *Little Women*. New York, New York: Signet Classic.

Altman, Alex. (2022). "A Syrian Refugee Story." Retrieved from *Time* magazine.

American Red Cross. (May 6, 2022). "American Red Cross Reaches 140 Years of Service, Innovation and Hope." Retrieved from the American Red Cross.

Carnegie Corporation of New York. (September 27, 2021). "15 Myths About Immigration Debunked." Retrieved from the Carnegie Corporation of New York.

Dvorak, Petula. (September 20, 2021). "Immigrants are there for these retirees. So the retirees decided to be there for them." Retrieved from *The Washington Post*.

Lingeman, Richard R. (April 30, 1978). "The Third Mr. Silverstein." Retrieved from *The New York Times*.

Perry, Tod. (April 8, 2022). "A new study completely debunks one of the worst stereotypes about immigrants." Retrieved from Upworthy.

Persecution International Christian Concern. (April 24, 2020). "Pakistan's Most Oppressed and the COVID-19 Pandemic." Retrieved from Persecution.org.

Szmigiera, M. (December 23, 2021). "Global Hunger Index 2021: countries most affected by hunger."

Teresa, Mother (1989). *No Greater Love*. Novato, California: New World Library.

Wohllenben, Peter. (2018). *The Hidden Life of Trees: The Illustrated Edition*. Vancouver: Greystone Books.

Zorn, Eric. (June 14, 2016). "Goofus, Gallant—the inside story." Retrieved from the *Chicago Tribune*.

ABOUT THE AUTHORS

Zach Zehnder is a husband, father, pastor, public speaker, and author. He is married to Allison, and they have two boys, Nathan and Brady. His life mission is to challenge people of all ages to become greater followers of Jesus. He is the Founder and President of Red Letter Living, author of the bestselling *Red Letter Challenge*, and host of the podcast *The Red Letter Disciple*. Zach has written or co-authored ten books that have helped people become greater followers of Jesus. Zach currently serves as Teaching Pastor at King of Kings in Omaha, NE. Zach is an experienced public speaker with a passion for making Jesus's name great. To book him for your conference, church, or event, go to www. redletterchallenge.com/zach.

Allison Zehnder was raised in Togo, West Africa, as a missionary kid. After moving back to the United States, she graduated from Concordia University Wisconsin with a degree in Theology and minor in Missions and Youth Ministry. After serving as Children's Director at theCross in Florida, Allison transitioned to writing full time for Red Letter Living. She is author of *Red Letter Challenge Kids, Being Challenge Kids, and Forgiving Challenge Kids.* She and Zach live in Elkhorn, NE, along with their sons, Nathan and Brady.

Doug Peterson is the Gold-Medallion-winning author of 79 books, including 42 for the popular VeggieTales series and six historical novels. He is the co-storywriter for the best-selling VeggieTales video, *Larry-Boy and the Rumor Weed,* and is currently working as head writer on a series of American history comic books. Doug has also been a writer for the University of Illinois since 1979, and he lives in Champaign, IL, with his wife, Nancy. They have two grown sons. You can find Doug online at bydougpeterson.com, or on Facebook under "Doug Peterson Author."

 FUN  INSPIRING  CRAZY  CHALLENGING

THE RED LETTER
DISCIPLE
WITH ZACH & CHRIS

The Red Letter Disciple is a podcast to help you become the greatest disciple of Jesus that you can possible be!

Learn more at:

WWW.REDLETTERPODCAST.COM

Subscribe or Follow:

Apple
Podcasts

YouTube

Spotify

JOIN THE RED LETTER COMMUNITY.

You don't have to follow Jesus alone! Commit today to a lifelong pursuit to follow Jesus.

Jump into the FREE Red Letter Community for ongoing discipleship challenges, brand new podcasts featuring world-class disciples, Jesus-centered blogs, Bible reading plans, and much, much more. Join today at:

WWW.REDLETTERCOMMUNITY.COM.

READY FOR
THE NEXT CHALLENGE?

40 DAYS TO BECOME A GREATER
DISCIPLE OF JESUS

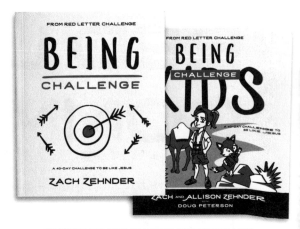

EXPERIENCE RAPID GROWTH IN
YOUR RELATIONSHIP WITH GOD
IN ONLY 40 DAYS

EXPERIENCE THE FREEDOM OF
GOD IN JUST 40 DAYS!

FIND OUT MORE AT
WWW.REDLETTERCHALLENGE.COM